Set the World on Fire

"Catholic retreats frequently focus a good deal on personal experience. A deficit of this approach is that reflecting on experience often requires the wisdom of the saints. In *Set the World on Fire*, Vinita Hampton Wright offers a subtle correction to this approach to retreats. Learning from four women masters of the spiritual tradition, as a retreatant you will cultivate a richer interior life through the myriad of spiritual exercises in this book. Whether you are doing this retreat all by yourself or in conversation with friends, if you are seeking to develop a spiritual life in the world, you will find *Set the World on Fire* a brilliant resource."

Timothy P. O'Malley
Author of *Real Presence*

"This book highlights the spirituality and brilliance of some of the most influential women in Church history. From the soaring visions of St. Hildegard to the little way of St. Thérèse, this retreat guides the reader in a simple yet profound reflection that will leave the soul refreshed and inspired."

Fr. Blake Britton
Contributor to Word on Fire Catholic Ministries

"Around the world, a hunger for a feminine Catholic voice is rising, and who better to pass the microphone to than the female doctors of the Church? Vinita Hampton Wright is the perfect retreat guide for this inner exploration, holding the brilliance of these four saints with the precision of an artist and the expansiveness of a spiritual director. This book is an important offering for those seeking authentic inner growth."

Shannon K. Evans
Author of *Embracing Weakness*

"Vinita Hampton Wright's latest book—written with her hallmark elegance, intelligence, and compassion—is a true gift. Not only does *Set the World on Fire* provide everything we could possibly need for a rich, self-guided meditative journey but it also invites us to participate in the intimate prayer lives of four spiritual giants of the Church, women whose visionary wisdom transformed Church doctrine."

Paula Huston
Author of *One Ordinary Sunday*

A 4-Week Personal Retreat
with the
Female Doctors of the Church

SET THE
WORLD
ON FIRE

Vinita Hampton Wright

AVE MARIA PRESS AVE Notre Dame, Indiana

© 2022 by Vinita Hampton Wright

All rights reserved. No part of this book may be used or reproduced in any manner whatsoever, except in the case of reprints in the context of reviews, without written permission from Ave Maria Press®, Inc., P.O. Box 428, Notre Dame, IN 46556, 1-800-282-1865.

Founded in 1865, Ave Maria Press is a ministry of the United States Province of Holy Cross.

www.avemariapress.com

Paperback: ISBN-13 978-1-64680-101-5

E-book: ISBN-13 978-1-64680-102-2

Cover image © Cecilia Lawrence.

Cover and text design by Samantha Watson.

Printed and bound in the United States of America.

Library of Congress Cataloging-in-Publication Data
Names: Wright, Vinita Hampton, 1958- author.
Title: Set the world on fire : a 4-week personal retreat with the female doctors of the church / Vinita Hampton Wright.
Description: Notre Dame, Indiana : Ave Maria Press, [2022] | Includes bibliographical references. | Summary: "This book uses a retreat format to study the four female doctors of the Church. It offers daily meditations, stories, and wisdom from lessons drawn from the lives of the Church's female visionaries"-- Provided by publisher.
Identifiers: LCCN 2021044387 (print) | LCCN 2021044388 (ebook) | ISBN 9781646801015 (paperback) | ISBN 9781646801022 (ebook)
Subjects: LCSH: Christian women saints. | Doctors of the church.
Classification: LCC BX4656 .W75 2022 (print) | LCC BX4656 (ebook) | DDC 235/.2082--dc23
LC record available at https://lccn.loc.gov/2021044387
LC ebook record available at https://lccn.loc.gov/2021044388

To every person who longs to welcome
Godself
and who hungers to find her or his true self
in the divine mystery

CONTENTS

TO BEGIN

*Be who God meant you to be, and you will
set the world on fire.*
—St. Catherine of Siena

You are about to spend four weeks with some extraordinary women:

o a young Carmelite nun whose autobiography sent ripples across Christendom and introduced us all to the little way

o another Carmelite who spent years reforming the order and gave to the world the spiritual masterpiece *The Interior Castle*

o a Third Order Dominican who poured out her life for people in need but also gave astute, sharp direction to Church leadership, including the pope

o a Benedictine abbess whose spiritual visions led to books, poetry, music, and early scientific discovery

The lives of these saints spanned eight centuries. Their experiences of God, their understanding of spirituality, and their timeless wisdom gained each the title Doctor of the Church—although that title, like their sainthood, was bestowed after death. While each woman lived day to day, she focused on deepening her relationship with God and living out what God called her to do and become.

Each woman brought to the Church multiple gifts, but we will concentrate on one emphasis for each in the weeks to come.

o St. Thérèse of Lisieux will show us how to love God through a little way.

o St. Teresa of Ávila will show us how to trust our personal experience of God.

o St. Catherine of Siena will show us how to grow in love and truth.

1

o   St. Hildegard of Bingen will show us how to engage life with great
    passion and creativity.

Saints and Doctors

Although each person in the family of God is considered a saint with a
small *s*, some people live in such a way that their imitation of Christ's love
has great impact on others. They are recognized in their own time as truly
holy. This holiness goes beyond the piety of saying prayers and maintaining
other spiritual practices; the holiness of a capital-*S* saint-in-the-making is
manifested in ministry to others. Such a saint relates to others in a truly
Christlike way: with humility, wisdom, passion, and a certain spiritual confidence that allows them to act on what they sense God is asking them to do.
Saints are brave but not haughty, resilient but not hardened. Saints often
suffer greatly, physically and otherwise.

Canonization is what we call the procedure that results in a person
being "made" a saint—that is, the process by which the Catholic Church
determines that a person should be designated as a saint. This takes a long
time, to allow for a thorough investigation. Sainthood requires proof that
at least two miracles have occurred that were the result of that person's
intercession. Also, it must be determined that the person's writings and
teachings contain no heresy. Technically, a person is declared venerable,
then is beatified, then finally is declared a saint.

A Doctor of the Church is the title applied to someone whose life work
has added significantly to the Church's understanding and practice of the
faith. This person's work is theologically sound and often theologically
expansive—that is, it deepens our understanding of God, ourselves, faith,
and the life of the Church. Also, the work is timeless, suited to the Church
during any age or circumstance. Pope John Paul II summarized this well
on the day he proclaimed St. Thérèse of Lisieux a Doctor of the Church:

> Indeed, when the Magisterium proclaims someone a doctor
> of the Church, it intends to point out to all the faithful,
> particularly to those who perform in the Church the funda-
> mental service of preaching or who undertake the delicate
> task of theological teaching and research, that the doctrine
> professed and proclaimed by a certain person can be a refer-
> ence point, not only because it conforms to revealed truth, but
> also because it sheds new light on the mysteries of the faith,

a deeper understanding of Christ's mystery. The Council reminded us that, with the help of the Holy Spirit, understanding of the "depositum fidei" continually grows in the Church, and not only does the richly contemplative study to which theologians are called, not only does the Magisterium of pastors, endowed with the "sure charism of truth," contribute to this growth process, but also that "*profound understanding of spiritual things*" which is given *through experience*, with the wealth and diversity of gifts, to all those who let themselves be docilely led by God's Spirit (cf. *Dei Verbum*, n. 8). *Lumen gentium*, for its part, teaches that God himself "speaks to us" (n. 50) in his saints. It is for this reason that the spiritual experience of the saints has a special value for deepening our knowledge of the divine mysteries, which remain ever greater than our thoughts, and not by chance does the Church choose only saints to be distinguished with the title of "doctor".[1]

Most Doctors of the Church are theologians to begin with, but in the cases of our four women—Thérèse, Teresa, Catherine, and Hildegard—their times and their gender meant teaching at theological institutions was unlikely. The fact that the Church has deemed these women Doctors of the Church highlights that the wisdom and generativity of their experience is as important as any academic accomplishment in the theological realm.

Why Spend These Weeks with Thérèse, Teresa, Catherine, and Hildegard?

Doctors of the Church receive that title because we believe their understanding of spirituality, theology, and the Church to be timeless and of great benefit to any generation and situation. These four doctors, being women from earlier times, bring to us additional spiritual sensibilities, such as experiencing God's presence in mundane work and growing spiritually without having any real power or authority in the world or the Church. We might argue that women also lend grounding to spiritual understanding because they have been so physically involved in bearing and raising children, nursing the sick and dying, and preparing food and medicine.

These four women will invite us to develop courage, humility, discernment, pragmatism, hope, joy, and vision. They will speak with words that go straight to our hearts and encourage us to widen our perceptions of living by faith and growing in love.

They have struggled, as we do.

They have overcome trials, as we do.

They have befriended God, as we endeavor to do.

They offer companionship as we grow in faith, hope, and love.

Through their distinctive gifts, these women became who God meant them to be, and each in her own way set the world on fire—with flames of love, wisdom, courage, and compassion.

They did not set out to be famous and have books written about them; they simply focused on loving God and allowing God's love to reach the world through their lives. They fought popular conventions, constant temptations, and a world of distractions to become lovers of God, followers of Jesus, and coworkers with the Holy Spirit.

These four women became what God intends for each of us. When you and I become free of sin, shame, and self-obsession, we can grow into our true selves. The Holy Spirit works within us to heal our wounds and dysfunctions and to strengthen us in all the virtues and gifts of the Spirit. We become functioning members of Christ's Body, people through whom God works to love others in tangible and transformative ways.

This is how the world is set on holy fire—flames of wisdom, justice, mercy, truth, beauty, and healing burn away the lies of the enemy and the damage of sin. We are called to be part of this redemptive process.

How to Use This Book

I have arranged the weeks not in the historical order of our saints but in the order their gifts might best benefit us. Thérèse will help us love God and others by small, steady steps. Teresa will encourage us to trust what God is doing, even when we don't understand it. Catherine will bolster our courage to use with confidence what God has given us. And Hildegard will nourish us as we delve into our own creativity.

Each week will begin with weekend reading and prayer, which will introduce the saint and the primary topic of the week. Following this will be five days of morning and evening prayer. Much of the text will come from the saint's own writings. Scripture, reflection questions, and suggestions for action will help you engage personally with the saint and her wisdom for living our faith.

Try to set aside enough time daily to linger with the saint and to allow the Holy Spirit to bring together her life with yours. There's no need to hurry, no mandate to work hard. Simply spend some time, open your heart, and invite the grace.

ST. THÉRÈSE OF LISIEUX, WHO SHOWS US HOW TO LOVE GOD THROUGH A LITTLE WAY

> If a little flower could speak, it seems to me
> that it would tell us quite simply all that
> God has done for it, without hiding any of
> its gifts. It would not, under the pretext of
> humility, say that it was not pretty, or that
> it had not a sweet scent, that the sun had
> withered its petals, or the storm bruised its
> stem, if it knew that such were not the case.
>
> — *Story of a Soul*[1]

This saint, the youngest Doctor of the Church, is known worldwide as the "Little Flower." She chose this simple image as the metaphor for her life. This metaphor speaks to what we know of her interior life: beauty, simplicity, humility, love. Most of us will never live in circumstances similar to hers, but we certainly can read her life as a story told for our benefit.

Week 1, Saturday

WHO WAS THÉRÈSE OF LISIEUX?

Marie Francois Thérèse Martin was born to very devout parents in 1873, the youngest of five surviving children. Her family life was filled with church activity and daily devotions, but Thérèse showed extraordinary spiritual aptitude even in that rich religious atmosphere. When Thérèse was four, her mother died, and Thérèse was cared for by her eldest sister, who eventually left home for the convent; the same happened with the next-eldest sister. By age fifteen, Thérèse felt called by God to enter the Carmelite order, but she was too young according to the convent rules. Thérèse appealed to the local bishop, who denied her. When she, her father, and remaining sister at home did pilgrimage in Rome, Thérèse then appealed to the pope. The girl was so insistent that she was allowed to enter the local convent after Lent—her sisters who were already nuns feared that the harsh fasting during Lent would be too hard on a fifteen-year-old.

Young Thérèse participated fully in the daily life of the Carmelite order. Many hours of prayer, times of solitude and contemplation, and physical work formed their days. Thérèse found it difficult to pray in community but took well to "mental" prayer—contemplation in silence and solitude. It was here that she encountered the God she had always longed after. It was to this God she brought her mundane trials and tribulations. As the somewhat spoiled baby of a family that had insulated her from the secular world, she was quite sensitive in nature. This tenderness of mind, emotion, and spirit was deepened by the multiple losses she had suffered so early in life: her mother to death and her two sister-mothers to their own vocations. Now, as the youngest in the convent, she had to deal with the hardships of an austere lifestyle as well as the undercurrents of emotional conflict that can develop in a closed and tightknit community of people who did not grow up together.

But Thérèse turned every form of suffering, small or great, into an opportunity to be unified even more with her "husband," Jesus. Carmelites consider themselves brides of Christ, and Thérèse's energy was focused on knowing Jesus better and loving him more. She also determined that, because she was so young and untrained in holiness, she would never be a great person of God. In the Lord's vast garden, all she could be was a "little flower." With such a limitation placed upon ambition, she was free to grow fully into who she was. Apparently, this was enough, because her spiritual maturity became evident to those around her.

When she contracted tuberculosis at age twenty-three, she accepted her fate as yet another way to be in communion with the God who loved her. In completing Christ's sufferings, she could further participate in the world's salvation.

During her dying months, Thérèse completed her life story, at the request of her Mother Superior. Today, we would consider it her memoir, and many people would scoff at the idea that a twenty-three-year-old would have lived long enough to have anything important to say. But in her few years, Thérèse had developed a depth of faith and love that few people attain over many decades. Her autobiography, *The Story of a Soul*, had traveled the world within a few years of her death. By 1923, she had been beatified, and she was made a saint in 1925. Pope John Paul II declared her a Doctor of the Church in 1997, with these words:

> Thérèse of the Child Jesus and the Holy Face is the young-est of all the "doctors of the Church", but her ardent spir-itual journey shows such maturity, and the insights of faith expressed in her writings are so vast and profound that they deserve a place among the great spiritual masters.
>
> In the Apostolic Letter which I wrote for this occasion, I stressed several salient aspects of her doctrine. But how can we fail to recall here what can be considered its high point, starting with the account of the moving discovery of her special vocation in the Church? "Charity", she wrote, "gave me the key to my vocation. I understood that if the Church had a body composed of different members, the most necessary and most noble of all could not be lacking to it, and so I understood that the Church had a heart and that this heart was burning with love. I understood that it was love alone that made the Church's members act, that if love were ever extinguished, apostles would not proclaim the Gospel and martyrs would refuse to shed their blood. I understood that love includes all vocations. . . . Then in the excess of my

delirious joy, I cried out: 'O Jesus, my Love . . . at last I have found my vocation; my vocation is Love!'" (*Ms B*, 3vº). This is a wonderful passage which suffices itself to show that one can apply to St Thérèse the Gospel passage we heard in the Liturgy of the Word: "I thank you Father, Lord of heaven and earth, that you have hidden these things from the wise and understanding and revealed them to babes" (Mt 11: 25).

Thérèse of Lisieux did not only grasp and describe the profound truth of Love as the center and heart of the Church, but in her short life she lived it intensely. It is precisely this *convergence of doctrine and concrete experience*, of truth and life, of teaching and practice, which shines with particular brightness in this saint, and which makes her an attractive model especially for young people and for those who are seeking true meaning for their life.[2]

On Thérèse's feast day in 2016, Pope Francis got to the heart of her life:

I would like to summarize these thoughts with some words from Saint Thérèse of the Child Jesus, whom we commemorate today. She shows her "little way" to God, "the trust of a little child who falls asleep without fear in his Father's arms", because "Jesus does not demand great actions from us, but simply surrender and gratitude" (*Autobiography*, Manuscript B, 1). Unfortunately, however, as she wrote then, and which still holds true today, God finds "few hearts who surrender to him without reservations, who understand the real tenderness of his infinite Love" (*ibid*). The young saint and Doctor of the Church, rather, was an expert in the "science of love" (*ibid*), and teaches us that "perfect charity consists in bearing with the faults of others, in not being surprised at their weakness, in being edified by the smallest acts of virtue we see them practice"; she reminds also that "charity cannot remain hidden in the depths our hearts" (*Autobiography*, Manuscript C, 12). Together let us all implore today the grace of a simple heart, of a heart that believes and lives in the gentle strength of love; let us ask to live in peaceful and complete trust in God's mercy.[3]

As we embark on this first week of prayer, we begin with a saint whose message bears much simplicity. Thérèse was religiously educated from early years but she did not have a scholastic education that would prepare her to write in esoteric theological terms. She speaks of daily events, personal struggles, the power of scripture, and the depth of her own desires. We can relate to her because of her honesty and directness. We can hope that those qualities in her will motivate us toward similar goals.

Get Ready

Here are some suggestions to prepare for the week:

○ Go online to do some research of your own on Thérèse of Lisieux. For instance, Fr. Robert Barron, "Saint Thérèse of Lisieux," July 6, 2015, YouTube video, 5:26, https://www.youtube.com/watch?v=03czgO8XUTg.

○ Compose three or four questions about your own life of prayer and activity. You can refer to these questions throughout the week as you read and pray.

Week 1, Sunday

PREPARATION

What do you find intriguing about St. Thérèse of Lisieux so far? What do you hope to learn from her?

Read the following gospel passage several times, noting words or phrases that stand out for you. Try to summarize in your own words what Jesus is doing. Imagine your reactions to him as if you were one of those traveling and ministering along with him.

Gospel for the Week: John 12:1–8

Six days before Passover Jesus came to Bethany, where Lazarus was, whom Jesus had raised from the dead. They gave a dinner for him there, and Martha served, while Lazarus was one of those reclining at table with him. Mary took a liter of costly perfumed oil made from genuine aromatic nard and anointed the feet of Jesus and dried them with her hair; the house was filled with the fragrance of the oil. Then Judas the Iscariot, one [of] his disciples, and the one who would betray him, said, "Why was this oil not sold for three hundred days' wages and given to the poor?" He said this not because he cared about the poor but because he was a thief and held the money bag and used to steal the contributions. So Jesus said, "Leave her alone. Let her keep this for the day of my burial. You always have the poor with you, but you do not always have me."

Inspiration from St. Thérèse

Just as the sun shines simultaneously on the tall cedars and on each little flower as though it were alone on the earth, so Our Lord is occupied particularly with each soul as though there were no others like it.

And just as in nature all the seasons are arranged in such a way as to make the humblest daisy bloom on a set day, in the same way, everything works out for the good of each soul.[4]

Prayer for the Week

Almighty God, Thérèse was able to receive your fatherly/ motherly love. May I come to that same willingness. Lord Jesus, our dear St. Thérèse centered on her love for you. May I develop more focus and intention in my relationship with you. Holy Spirit, you worked great holiness in St. Thérèse because she truly desired God and had a humble perception of herself. Teach me to discern my true desires and to assess myself with truth and humility. Amen.

Week 1, Monday

THE WAY OF PRAYER

Morning Prayer

Scripture: Psalm 141:2

Let my prayer be counted as incense before you,
And the lifting up of my hands as an evening sacrifice.

Thérèse entered the Carmelites quite young: age fifteen. The lifestyle was demanding enough for older women—silence, daily manual labor, the isolation of the cloister, and the endless cycles of prayer. Thérèse struggled to focus when doing traditionally spoken prayer such as the Rosary or even the Our Father. Given that the Carmelites followed the prayers of the Divine Hours, Thérèse must have been frustrated on a regular basis, trying to repeat the prayers meaningfully. She was naturally drawn to mental prayer, which was more interior and free-flowing. It's not surprising that she came to the following conclusion.

From St. Thérèse

For me, prayer is an upward rising of the heart, it's a simple glance toward heaven, it's a cry of gratitude and love in the midst of trials as much as in the midst of joys. In short, it's something big, something great, something supernatural that expands my heart and unites me to Jesus.[5]

Read this quote of Thérèse's and note any word or image that stands out for you. I've always loved the phrase "simple glance toward heaven" because it presents prayer as something that comes naturally, that isn't hard work. What image or word appeals to you, and why?

Read the prayer a second time. Is there any part of it you sense God is speaking to you personally right now? Write it down and speak it aloud a few times.

Read it a third time. How do you sense yourself responding to this prayer? To the part God is speaking to you?

Ask Some Questions

1. What kind of prayer comes most easily to you?

    As a writer—a word person—I pray quite naturally with words, especially those beautifully written, such as a psalm or poem. I have also found singing to be a natural form of prayer because I've sung since early childhood. What comes naturally to you as you approach communion with God?

    What has made prayer comfortable for you in the past? What attracts you to prayer now?

2. When am I most likely to feel a comfortable flow to my prayer?

    Some people just don't do well sitting still—they pray much more easily while walking, for instance. In my work as a spiritual director, I try to help people understand what feels right to them as they approach prayer. Some people need to kneel or stand up with hands raised. Others need a quiet and very private place. What about you?

3. In what ways does my heart "rise" during a typical day?

    Can I identify such a time recently?

    Don't assume that a rising heart happens only in moments of calm or contentment. My heart rises most naturally when I am in deep sorrow and crying out for help. You will most likely find your heart rising to God when you understand that God is not judging you or being angry with you. Our rising to God signals an expectation of acceptance and love. When are you most inclined to expect God's generosity and care?

A Practice

Today, pray in a way that flows well for you: a memorized prayer such as the Our Father, an imagined conversation with Jesus, some quiet time to notice God's presence, journaling about what you're grateful for—whatever form of prayer that works best.

Closing Prayer

Lord Jesus, you helped Thérèse recognize what prayer truly was for her. Open my eyes and my heart to the forms of prayer that are your gifts to me. Amen.

Evening Prayer

o   I take a few deep, slow breaths and invite the Holy Spirit to help me pray.

o   To do with my body what I hope to do with my spirit, I sit up (or stand), lift my face to the sky, and open my arms. And I pray: Loving God, I lift my heart, my mind, my soul—my whole self to you. You know my every hope and fear, pain and pleasure, dream and burden. I lift all of it into your shining love and grace. Amen.

Prayer to St. Thérèse

St. Thérèse, help me to always believe as you did in God's great love for me, so that I might imitate your little way each day. Amen.

Scripture: Psalm 121

I lift up my eyes to the hills—
  from where will my help come?
My help comes from the LORD,
  who made heaven and earth.
He will not let your foot be moved;
  he who keeps you will not slumber.
He who keeps Israel
  will neither slumber nor sleep.
The LORD is your keeper;
  the LORD is your shade at your right hand.
The sun shall not strike you by day,
  nor the moon by night.
The LORD will keep you from all evil;
  he will keep your life.
The LORD will keep
  your going out and your coming in
  from this time on and for evermore.

Look for Growth

What might happen when I lift my eyes and heart to God?

o   I focus on God, not myself or my situation.
o   I open the eyes of my heart and look for God, increasing my ability to recognize God.
o   I glance upward in gratitude and hope rather than downward in bitterness and fear.
o   I widen my vision and expand my spiritual capacity.

o   I increase my faith because I am seeking God's presence.

Prayer from, or Inspired by, St. Thérèse

When comes the evening of life, I shall stand before Thee with empty hands, because I do not ask Thee, my God, to take account of my works. All our works of justice are blemished in Thine Eyes. I wish therefore to be robed with Thine own Justice, and to receive from Thy Love the everlasting gift of Thyself. I desire no other Throne, no other Crown but Thee, O my Beloved! In Thy sight time is naught—"one day is a thousand years." Thou canst in a single instant prepare me to appear before Thee.[6]

Gospel Sentence: Mark 1:35

Rising very early before dawn, he left and went off to a deserted place, where he prayed.

It can be quite helpful to review your prayer once you've finished. For instance, I might journal after my evening prayer, something like, "I'm grateful that opening my hands during prayer felt so natural. Maybe I should do that more often. I think it puts me into a more receptive mode in general."

Or another review of my prayer might be: "I was so distracted this evening. Nothing was 'rising' or 'lifting'—I'm sorry, Lord. But I trust that you receive whatever I have."

Week 1, Tuesday

THE WAY OF CHILDLIKENESS

Morning Prayer

Scripture: Isaiah 66:12–13

[Y]ou shall nurse and be carried on her arm,
   and dandled on her knees.
As a mother comforts her child,
   so I will comfort you;
   you shall be comforted in Jerusalem.

Thérèse was little more than a child when she decided to become a Carmelite—and she was barely past childhood when given permission to join a convent. She recognized how she seemed to others who considered her spoiled, not serious about the religious life, unable to appreciate what such a commitment truly meant.

You would think that she would work hard at leaving childhood behind and act as grown-up as possible; that she would resist childhood images in her prayers and meditations—after all, she had so much to prove to those older nuns, some of whom did not hide their uncharitable attitudes toward her.

Yet her prayer and experience brought her to treasure the Isaiah picture of a nursing babe.

From St. Thérèse

Oh! Never have words more tender, more melodious, come to rejoice my soul. The elevator that must lift me up to heaven is Your arms, Jesus! For that I don't need to become big. On the contrary, I have to stay little—may I become little, more and more.

God, You have surpassed my expectations, and I want to sing of Your mercies. "Since my youth, God, you have taught me, and to this

day I declare your marvelous deeds. Even when I am old and gray,
do not forsake me, my God." [Psalm 71:17–18] When will be my time
of being "old and gray"? It seems to me that it could be now, because
2,000 years are not more in the Lord's eyes than twenty years.[7]

God's presence and action in a person's life transcends age, years, maturity, or anyone's perception of the person. A very young person can be "old and gray" in the sense of an active and developing faith, just as an elderly person can remain cynical and petulant, refusing to grow in faith, love, or hope.

And our perception of ourselves—and others' perceptions of us—are entirely overrated in God's universe of timelessness and grace. How much energy have I spent trying to maintain the appearance of being mature or wise? How often have I suffered embarrassment upon remembering the faith of my youth—even though it was true faith and pleasing to God despite its lack of experience or depth?

Perhaps when Jesus said we must have the faith of a child, he was thinking of our self-conscious efforts at being "grown-ups"—strong, smart, self-sufficient, correct in our beliefs—rather than simple acceptance of ourselves as loved and the willingness to turn to that love and rely on it.

Ask Some Questions

1. How conscious am I of others' opinions of me, especially my faith life?
    How much do I think about what others think?
    When have I spoken or acted a certain way because I was playing to an imagined audience?

2. When was the last time I allowed myself to be helped, held, comforted, guided?

    How did I feel to receive any of those things?

    Did I welcome what was offered or did I try to resist it?

    Did I feel guilty for needing what was given?

    Was I embarrassed that I needed anything from anyone?

3. How important is it to me to be knowledgeable about faith and mature in its practice?

    How much space do I give myself to develop maturity over time?

    How patient am I with the slow and gradual process of interior growth?

A Practice

Try to connect with any feeling of need you have today: for help, comfort, protection, assurance, courage, and so on. Ask the Holy Spirit to show you your need.

Go to your bedroom or another place where you can lie down in privacy and quiet. Curl up in that spot and ask God to hold you. As you remain in that position for a while, say plainly what you need. (God, I feel so discouraged today. Lord, I'm scared—I know I shouldn't be, but I am. Holy Mother, I miss my daughter, who's away at school and is too busy to call me. Dear Jesus, I don't know what to do—please show me.)

Closing Prayer

Dear Heavenly Father, I think of you so often as a father that I forget all those motherly qualities named in the scriptures. I need to feel your motherly presence today. Help me become childlike in my ability to come to you for what I need and snuggle into the grace you offer. Amen.

Evening Prayer

- o I take a few deep, slow breaths and invite the Holy Spirit to help me pray.
- o To do with my body what I hope to do with my spirit, I sit up (or stand), lift my face to the sky, and open my arms. And I pray: Heavenly Father/ Mother, just as any parent desires to check in with a son or daughter— child or adult—at the end of the day, I believe you want to check in with me. Here I am! Amen.

Prayer to St. Thérèse

Dear Thérèse, pray for me as I seek to pray as a loved child speaks to her parent. Amen.

Scripture: Romans 8:14–16

For all who are led by the Spirit of God are children of God. For you did not receive a spirit of slavery to fall back into fear, but you have received a spirit of adoption. When we cry, "Abba! Father!" it is that very Spirit bearing witness with our spirit that we are children of God.

Look for Growth

What might happen when I allow God to hold me like a small child?

o   I connect with my true needs in this moment.
o   I remember God's tender love and thus reject the temptation to fear God as one who would shame or condemn me.
o   My interior needs merge with my memories of being small and my physical sense of being in the presence of an infinitely greater One who loves me.
o   Divine love has the opportunity to deepen my sense of trust and of God's nearness.

Prayer from, or Inspired by, St. Thérèse

O Jesus, dear Holy Child, my only treasure, I abandon myself to Thy every whim. I seek no other joy than that of calling forth Thy sweet Smile. Vouchsafe to me the graces and the virtues of Thy Holy Childhood, so that on the day of my birth into Heaven the Angels and Saints may recognize in Thy Spouse: Teresa of the Child Jesus.[8]

Gospel Sentence: Matthew 23:37

Jerusalem, Jerusalem, you who kill the prophets and stone those sent to you, how many times I yearned to gather your children together, as a hen gathers her young under her wings, but you were unwilling!

I confess that as one who awakened to God's presence as a child, I have struggled to accept my various stages of spiritual development, especially when I look back at them. I was a child who thought of God and Jesus in almost magical terms (typical in children); I was the adolescent who transferred my needs for acceptance onto a savior whom I wanted to be my best friend and defender against kids who didn't like me; I was the zealous college student who had more answers than questions; and so on. I would look back at each previous stage and want to erase all of it and accept as reality only the present version of myself. It has been a self-conscious and often counterproductive way to live.

Thérèse had a short life in chronological terms and was never physically old enough to be seen by many people as a person of well-developed faith and spiritual practice. She reminds us of many young people who die before coming into full bloom, or so it seems. Can we entertain the possibility that God has little if any concern for our chronology? Is it possible that our Lord sees us always as eternal, as present tense forever, as fully formed even while we are forming? In considering these possibilities, we are entering a mystical aspect of our life with God. Perhaps Thérèse was traversing mystical territory at times, but her own words describe an almost simple celebration of a growing sense of God's tender love. She discovered more and more that she was loved dearly and always. And she learned more and more to receive it and rejoice.

Week 1, Wednesday

THE WAY OF SUFFERING

Morning Prayer

Scripture: Isaiah 53:2

For he grew up before him like a young plant,
  and like a root out of dry ground;
he had no form or majesty that we should look at him,
  nothing in his appearance that we should desire him.

When scholars and theologians discuss this young Carmelite Doctor of the Church, they inevitably come to Thérèse's theology of suffering. She experienced obvious pain and loss from early childhood: the death of her mother and the departure of the sisters who had become her caregivers and companions when they left to their own religious vocations before her. Then, the acute illness that attacked when she was in her early twenties and took her life by age twenty-four. In her final months, probably due in part to severe physical suffering, she endured spiritual darkness and doubt.

In addition, the Catholic Church and culture that shaped Thérèse's family and social existence was trudging through fires of its own during the bloody French Revolution and its aftermath; a good Catholic in Thérèse's era considered martyrdom not only an honorable outcome but a likely one as well. Suffering was expected of God's people, and the young Thérèse approached suffering as part of what she owed Christ who had suffered for her. She began with an attitude of duty to her God, which included the willingness to embrace suffering so that souls might be saved and the godless world outside might be set right.

But personal theology nearly always evolves and changes as gritty experience shapes one's day-to-day sensibilities. As Thérèse was drawn into Jesus' fervent love and presence, she came to attach every aspect of her life to that ongoing reality. Along with many other Catholics, Thérèse was devoted to the Holy Face of Christ—in fact, her full name upon taking the veil was Thérèse of the Child Jesus and the Holy Face. But what began as a traditional devotion, focused on payment for the world's sin and unbelief, for Thérèse became yet another point of contact with the Jesus she loved. She contemplated the face of her suffering savior and encountered there the homely love foreshadowed in the Isaiah passage. Thus, even suffering became a means of being with Jesus—relating to him, accompanying him, encountering him in the intimacy of pain that strips a person to the bones of their soul. Once again, love overwhelmed and transformed what began as mere religion. In the words of Elizabeth A. Dreyer, "She begins as a scrupulous judgmental, petulant individual and ends in utter simplicity and loving surrender."[9]

From St. Thérèse

The little flower that was transplanted onto the mountain of Carmel was destined to open in the shadow of the Cross. The tears and the blood of Jesus became the dew that watered it, and its Sun was His Adorable Face veiled with tears. . . . Until then I hadn't plumbed the depths of the treasures hidden in the Holy Face of Jesus. It was through you, dear Mother, that I learned to know them. Just as you had once gone before us all to Carmel, in the same way you were the first to penetrate the mysteries of love hidden in the Countenance of our Bridegroom. Then you called me, and I understood. . . . I understood what was the *real glory*. The one whose kingdom is not of this world showed me that true wisdom consists in "wanting to be unknown and counted as nothing, in placing one's joy in disdain for oneself." Oh! Like Jesus' face, I wanted "My face to be truly hidden that on earth no one should recognize me." I was thirsty for suffering and for being forgotten. . . .

How merciful is the path along which God has always led me. He never made me desire anything without giving it to me, so His bitter cup seemed delicious to me.[10]

Ask Some Questions

1. How was I taught to think about suffering and hardship in my family of origin?

    In my faith community (if I had one)?

    What conversations about suffering can I remember taking place among friends when I was in high school and/or college?

2. What is the purpose of suffering, as I understand it now?
        Or do I believe it has a purpose?
        What does suffering have to do with God's will and with how God
    deals with me in daily life?

3. Do I have a theology of suffering?
        If so, what is it? Can I trace its development?
        Has it remained static or changed over my life so far—and if so,
    how has it changed?

A Practice

Thérèse endured loss and pain during childhood. Also, when she was at
boarding school, when she struggled to convince authorities to give her
permission to join the convent, when she was learning the life of a Carmelite sister, and on and on, she felt awkward and isolated. Each phase of her
life brought its trials, and those brought her closer to God.

Sketch out major seasons in your own life and identify the suffering in
each.

Ask Jesus to meet you in each memory and help you better understand how suffering wove into who you were and what you were learning.

Have the courage to talk honestly with God about the pain in those various periods of your life.

Closing Prayer

Lord Jesus, my life may not have much in common with Thérèse's life, but I have suffered. Help me call to mind the griefs I've endured, the pain that has washed over me, sometimes threatening to drown my faith. Help me give words to that suffering now and talk with you about it. Amen.

Evening Prayer

○ I take a few deep, slow breaths and invite the Holy Spirit to help me pray.

○ To do with my body what I hope to do with my spirit, I sit up (or stand), lift my face to the sky, and open my arms. And I pray: Lord Jesus, draw me to the moments of your Passion and death. Help me linger with you and gaze upon your face, taking in your pain but also the love that bore it.

Prayer to St. Thérèse

St. Thérèse, you learned to perceive everything—even your pain—through the loving gaze of Jesus. Help me develop this spiritual grace.

Scripture: 2 Corinthians 4:8–11

We are afflicted in every way, but not crushed; perplexed, but not driven to despair; persecuted, but not forsaken; struck down, but not destroyed; always carrying in the body the death of Jesus, so that the life of Jesus may also be made visible in our bodies. For while we live, we are always being given up to death for Jesus' sake, so that the life of Jesus may be made visible in our mortal flesh.

Look for Growth

What might happen when I meditate and gaze upon Jesus' suffering?

o   I confront his humanity. He felt pain, loss, hunger, grief just as I do.
o   These moments open something deeper in Jesus' suffering; I begin to see an underlying intent and plan—a purpose even—in life's harsh experiences.
o   I begin to understand that Jesus—Lord of all creation—takes comfort in my being with him in these horrific moments. *I* have something to offer the Son of God.
o   My own pain gradually melts into a much larger pool of what I can only call the world's pain. I am not alone, and somehow that makes a difference.

Prayer from, or Inspired by, St. Thérèse

I thank You, O my God, for all the graces You have granted me: especially for having purified me in the crucible of suffering. At the Day of Judgment I shall gaze on You with joy, as You bear Your scepter of the Cross. And since You have given me this precious Cross as my portion, I hope to be like You in Paradise and to behold the Sacred Wounds of Your Passion shine on my glorified body.[11]

Gospel Sentence: Luke 9:23

Then he said to all, "If anyone wishes to come after me, he must deny himself and take up his cross daily and follow me."

We may not think that we have a "theology of suffering," but we have acquired bits and pieces of belief about it from our earliest days. Consciously or not, we act out a theology. It is a task of spiritual maturity to identify all those bits and pieces and reckon with them. Nearly always we have picked up some toxic material along the way.

When I was in high school, a man in our community was killed in a car accident. A local preacher told the man's teenage son that his wayward actions were no doubt partly responsible for this evil befalling the family. He was teaching the theology of suffering as payback for our sins. You likely have some stories of your own, of harmful beliefs being foisted on someone during a time of suffering—for example, a loved one would be healed of cancer if only they had enough faith. There was some unconfessed sin at the bottom of this tragedy. God is trying to get your attention—that's why that awful thing was allowed to happen.

But Thérèse would, in this time and place, offer an extraordinary message: This pain can become a portal to pure, powerful, joyful love. It may take time, but if you keep peering into this darkness, you will find yourself gazing into Jesus' eyes. And those eyes hold your pain. They welcome you. That loving gaze will hold you firmly and help you find your way.

Week 1, Thursday

THE WAY OF HUMILITY

Morning Prayer

Scripture: Philippians 2:3-4

> Do nothing from selfish ambition or conceit, but in humility regard others as better than yourselves. Let each of you look not to your own interests, but to the interests of others.

Perhaps because Thérèse was sensitive to begin with and had a history of reacting strongly to even small disappointments and slights, she made a point to seek humility in her life as a nun. Certainly, enough irritations and slights occurred in daily community life. Thérèse focused on humility in her prayers and denied herself even the right to correct someone's wrong assumptions about her. She was the youngest person in the community and came from a quite sheltered existence; it's likely that some of the older nuns considered her a bit too precious or pious, that they, at least in the beginning, did not give her much credit or think she was genuine. Over time, though, they came to see that this young woman was serious about her vocation. But Thérèse did not concern herself with what they thought but sought to emulate the humility and meekness of Jesus.

From Thérèse

> The one thing which is not open to envy is the lowest place. Here alone, therefore, there is neither vanity nor affliction of spirit. Yet, "the way of a man is not his own," and sometimes we find ourselves wishing for what dazzles. In that hour let us in all humility take our place among the imperfect, and look upon ourselves as little souls who at every instant need to be upheld by the goodness of God. From the moment He sees us fully convinced of our nothingness, and hears us cry out: "My foot stumbles, Lord, but Thy Mercy is my strength,"
>
> He reaches out His Hand to us. But, should we attempt great things, even under pretext of zeal, He deserts us. It suffices,

> therefore, to humble ourselves, to bear with meekness our imper-
> fections. Herein lies—for us—true holiness.[12]

It's most difficult to remain humble when others don't "get" us, isn't it? When their ideas about us are misinformed or based on false assumptions. Something in us demands for the record to be set straight. We think of humility being primarily the way people think about themselves, but I have found that I struggle most with humility when it comes to how others perceive me. It's extremely important that people not get the wrong impression. And when someone questions my motives or attributes to me motives that are not true, my anger is almost instantaneous.

True humility is not being invested in my reputation or worried about others getting the wrong idea or not understanding me accurately enough. True humility focuses on what is going on between God and me; what others do with that should simply be none of my concern.

Ask Some Questions

1. What is my own working definition of *humility*?
    How did that definition develop?

2. When am I most likely to take offense, in terms of how others treat me? What triggers my anger—or my shame?

3. Looking at some of my key relationships, what would humility look like in my words and actions on a typical day?

    How might I react differently to people if I left my honor up to Jesus?

A Practice

Ask the Holy Spirit to bring to your memory one or two events in which you observed true humility in someone else. What happened, and how did that person respond? How did that event affect you at the time?

Also recall a time when you were aware that you were facing a choice between pride and humility. What was happening, and what did you do?

Closing Prayer

Lord Jesus, I think you could be humble because you had such a strong sense of who you truly were—God's beloved. You needed no more honor than that. Help me be satisfied with my glorious status as one who is beloved of God—so that I can let go of pride and stop worrying about my "status."

Evening Prayer

- o I take a few deep, slow breaths and invite the Holy Spirit to help me pray.
- o To do with my body what I hope to do with my spirit, I sit up (or stand), lift my face to the sky, and open my arms. And I pray: Lord, I'm not terribly attracted to humility, but you already know that, don't you? Help me desire a humble heart.

Prayer to St. Thérèse

St. Thérèse, even as you were dying, you planned to continue helping us from heaven. Help me be brave enough to invite genuine humility to take root in my heart. Amen.

Scripture 1 Peter 5:6–7

Humble yourselves therefore under the mighty hand of God, so that
he may exalt you in due time. Cast all your anxiety on him, because
he cares for you.

Look for Growth

What might happen when I grow in humility?

o   A lot of stress will melt away because I won't be constantly worrying
    about how I look to others.
o   By taking myself out of the center of my vision, I will see others more
    clearly and empathetically.
o   I will be in a much better position to learn from Jesus, who is meek
    and humble of heart.
o   Other people will see me not as a threat but as someone with whom
    they are safe and loved.

Prayer from, or Inspired by, St. Thérèse

I implore you, dear Jesus, to send me a humiliation whenever
I try to set myself above others.

And yet, dear Lord, you know my weakness. Each morning I resolve to be humble, and in the evening I recognize
that I have often been guilty of pride. The sight of these faults
tempts me to discouragement; yet I know that discouragement is itself but a form of pride. I wish, therefore, O my God,
to build all my trust upon you. As you can do all things, plant
in my soul this virtue which I desire, and to obtain it from
your infinite mercy, I will often say to you: "Jesus, meek and
humble of heart, make my heart like yours."[13]

Gospel Sentence: Luke 14:11

For everyone who exalts himself will be humbled, but the one who humbles himself will be exalted.

Every now and then—but probably not often enough—it occurs to me how much easier life would become if I didn't think about myself so much. Whether obsessed with my hair or worried about how I came across in a conversation, I feel an old weariness creep in: I am so tired of myself.

God's desire for us is perfect freedom. When we are free of sin, anxiety, fear, and self-centeredness, we can enjoy the grace that showers upon us every moment. Working constantly at the self and all its "improvements" becomes a drain on the life that could be contented and at ease.

And can you imagine the freedom of not worrying about my position and reputation? Not having to dominate how a conversation goes or guide how a plan comes together? In typical human interactions there is always some version of politicking, of power plays and shows of strength. Thérèse tried to detach herself from all of that—not because she thought of herself as worthless but because she understood herself to be loved by God and that every other relationship in her life was to grow out of that communion.

Humility can look like powerlessness because it often involves relinquishing power. But true humility frees us to be who we are in Christ. We need not strive to be anything else.

Week 1, Friday

THE WAY OF
TOTAL LONGING

Morning Prayer

Scripture: Psalm 42:1-3

As a deer longs for flowing streams,
    so my soul longs for you, O God.
My soul thirsts for God,
    for the living God.
When shall I come and behold
    the face of God?
My tears have been my food
    day and night,
while people say to me continually,
    "Where is your God?"

I've often thought that God chose Mary of Nazareth to be the mother of Jesus because she was a young girl, and the passion and longing of a woman in her early teens cannot be matched. Those of us who have girls that age in our families know that once an idea takes hold, there's no telling how many hours will be given to a project and how much energy will go to a cause.

Thérèse of Lisieux may have been sheltered and sensitive, but she had the gift of longing, and she allowed that longing to stimulate her to prayer and action. When, at age fifteen, she had an audience with the pope, her longing caused her to violate protocol and speak to the pope, reach out to him, and make her case to become a nun—until the guards had to remove her physically. After she entered the Carmelite convent in Lisieux, her longing carried her through the hardship and discipline, through limitations and frequent illness. Rather than decrease in the face of these challenges, her longing for God just kept growing. She let it flourish in her heart and in her words.

From St. Thérèse

O my Beloved! this was but the prelude of graces yet greater which Thou didst desire to heap upon me. Let me remind Thee of them to-day, and forgive my folly if I venture to tell Thee once more of my hopes, and my heart's well nigh infinite longings—forgive me and grant my desire, that it may be well with my soul. To be Thy Spouse, O my Jesus, to be a daughter of Carmel, and by my union with Thee to be the mother of souls, should not all this content me? And yet other vocations make themselves felt—I feel called to the Priesthood and to the Apostolate—I would be a Martyr, a Doctor of the Church. I should like to accomplish the most heroic deeds—the spirit of the Crusader burns within me, and I long to die on the field of battle in defence of Holy Church.

The vocation of a Priest! With what love, my Jesus, would I bear Thee in my hand, when my words brought Thee down from Heaven! With what love would I give Thee to souls! And yet, while longing to be a Priest, I admire and envy the humility of St. Francis of Assisi, and am drawn to imitate him by refusing the sublime dignity of the Priesthood. How reconcile these opposite tendencies?

Like the Prophets and Doctors, I would be a light unto souls, I would travel to every land to preach Thy name, O my Beloved, and raise on heathen soil the glorious standard of Thy Cross. One mission alone would not satisfy my longings. I would spread the Gospel to the ends of the earth, even to the most distant isles. I would be a Missionary, not for a few years only, but, were it possible, from the beginning of the world till the consummation of time. Above all, I thirst for the Martyr's crown. It was the desire of my earliest days, and the desire has deepened with the years passed in the Carmel's narrow cell. But this too is folly, since I do not sigh for one torment; I need them all to slake my thirst. Like Thee, O Adorable Spouse, I would be scourged, I would be crucified! I would be flayed like St. Bartholomew, plunged into boiling oil like St. John, or, like St. Ignatius of Antioch, ground by the teeth of wild beasts into a bread worthy of God.[14]

Wow! Little Thérèse wanted it all! To be the spouse of Christ, to be a priest, a missionary, a martyr. She unashamedly poured out these desires. Would she be granted any of these things? Surely she knew not to expect priesthood, and I doubt she expected a missionary life, given her frail physical state. It was not unusual for religious men and women to honor martyrdom, to even want it.

But it seems not to have mattered so much what the outcome would be. Thérèse poured out her desires in her conversations with God, trusting that God would do with them whatever God chose. Her part was simply to desire all the graces God might have to offer.

Ask Some Questions

1. When have I longed for something, really longed for it to the point of expressing that desire to God?

2. Am I usually aware of my heart desires or do I not think of them much?
   If I don't think of them, why is that?
   Do I not express desires that I think may not come to fruition?

3.   What desires in my life might be concealing deeper, truer desires?
     That is, do I spend more thought and energy on desires about
     clothing, food, work, and daily matters than I do on the more profound
     desires for love, purpose, and peace?
     What do I do with those deeper desires?

A Practice

If you're a writer, then open your journal; if you prefer images, then
prepare your blank page and pencils or paints. Give yourself at least a
half hour to express what you long for most.

Closing Prayer

We long for you, O God,

because we are designed to house your glorious life.

Our ache is answered by your grace.

Our desire has hollowed out a space inside

that fits your love precisely.

May we welcome you for whom

our souls have cried. Amen.

Evening Prayer

o   I take a few deep, slow breaths and invite the Holy Spirit to help me pray.

o   To do with my body what I hope to do with my spirit, I sit up (or stand), lift my face to the sky, and open my arms. And I pray: Give me the courage, Lord God, to look into my soul and see what is missing.

Prayer to St. Thérèse

Dear Thérèse, you were so willing to be needy! So happy to run to the Lord you loved. Run with me now, toward the longing in me that needs to be heard, so that I can speak that longing into God's listening ear. Amen.

Scripture: John 4:7–15

A Samaritan woman came to draw water, and Jesus said to her, "Give me a drink." His disciples had gone to the city to buy food. The Samaritan woman said to him, "How can you, a Jew, ask me, a Samaritan woman, for a drink?" (For Jews use nothing common with Samaritans.) Jesus answered and said to her, "If you knew the gift of God and who is saying to you, 'Give me a drink,' you would have asked him and he would have given you living water." [The woman] said to him, "Sir, you do not even have a bucket and the well is deep; where then can you get this living water? Are you greater than our father Jacob, who gave us the well and drank from it himself with his children and his flocks?" Jesus answered and said to her, "Everyone who drinks of this water will be thirsty again; but whoever drinks the water I shall give will become in him a spring of water welling up to eternal life." The woman said to him, "Sir, give me this water, so that I may not be thirsty or have to keep coming here to draw water."

Look for Growth

What might happen if I allowed myself to connect with my truest desires?

- ○ I would let go of more superficial matters.
- ○ My prayer would become more honest and meaningful.
- ○ I would begin to form my life around what is most important.
- ○ I would open a new channel of communication between myself and God.

Prayer from, or Inspired by, St. Thérèse

Lord Jesus, may my heart open to you completely,

may my desires for you only increase,

and may my joy in your presence endure

through every circumstance. Amen.

Gospel Sentence: Matthew 7:7–8

Ask and it will be given to you; seek and you will find; knock and the door will be opened to you. For everyone who asks, receives; and the one who seeks, finds; and to the one who knocks, the door will be opened.

It's not unusual for people to shy away from their own desires, even fear them. Yet throughout the Bible we see God's pleasure at people's requests and their expressions of longing. Can you think of a single time in scripture when God said something like, "Stop asking for things! I don't want to hear about what you want or need!" On the contrary, God waits for our engagement and listens for our prayers. Thérèse believed this and simply prayed from her longings. She didn't expect them to all "come true," as though God were granting wishes. To her, these prayers of longing were expressions of her love for God; her desires were just one facet of her ongoing conversation with Jesus.

The story of the woman at the well indicates that our thirst is there for a reason: when we attend to it, the thirst itself will bring us to Jesus, that everlasting water. Will we sometimes long for something that isn't right for us or not meant for us? Of course—just as Thérèse desired to be a priest, missionary, martyr. Desire will set us in motion, and once in motion, we can be guided in more detail by the Holy Spirit. The greater danger is not to move at all, not to acknowledge that we are hungry, thirsty, weary, needing justice. Without our longings, would we go on journeys, look for answers, try to learn or discover? Desire—thirst, hunger, longing—fuels our interior movement and always draws us to our Source.

Thérèse's Fire

This young woman poured out her love to God and walked her little way to do whatever God's will was for her life. The result? Her story and her words have traveled the world, kindling in others the courage to follow their hearts right to Jesus and to live out that love in everyday life.

What is your little way? How does your specific life connect with Jesus' mission to reconcile the whole world to God, to love others in such a way that they desire to know Jesus too?

ST. TERESA OF ÁVILA, WHO ENCOURAGES US TO OWN OUR UNIQUE LIFE WITH GOD

Let nothing bother you,
Let nothing scare you.
Everything changes,
Always.
Only God is steady and changeless.

But patience hits the target.
Only patience always gets what it wants.
The person who possesses God possesses everything.
That person lacks nothing.
Only God satisfies your every need.

—*Prayers*[1]

Many of us have heard some version of this famous prayer. I chose Carmen Acevedo Butcher's translation for its fresh wording that a twenty-first-century person might relate to. In this prayer we are urged to take ourselves in hand—"Let nothing bother you"—and to be patient. We are reminded that God satisfies our every need. I feel some tension; perhaps you do too. It's not enough for me simply to trust God. This relationship is anything but passive on my part. Clearly, in this spiritual life, I have work to do. I can sense St. Teresa nodding as I write this.

Week 2, Saturday

WHO WAS TERESA OF ÁVILA?

Teresa was born in Ávila in 1515 to a family with Jewish roots: her father's father was a Jew, and persecution had sent the family to Ávila years before. Teresa's childhood was happy and secure, and she had an attractive and outgoing nature. Ultimately, though, she chose a religious life over marriage, against her father's wishes, and joined the Carmelite Convent of the Incarnation when she was twenty-one. This life of prayer was not easy for her, and her mystical experiences of God, which elicited doubts and accusations in her community, impressed a certain isolation upon her. Teresa's peculiar life of prayer, coupled with serious and chronic illness, created a unique spiritual path for her that required courage, perseverance, and faith that clung to the God who drew her and loved her.

In the end, she became a powerful communicator, an administrator who created convents across Spain, a reformer of the Carmelite order, and the writer of spiritual works that, although intended for the welfare of the nuns she supervised, broke out of the convent to touch the lives of religious and laypeople in her lifetime and in the centuries since.

Teresa of Ávila was the first woman to be named a Doctor of the Church; this happened under Pope Paul VI in 1970. After nearly five centuries, the most authoritative voices in the Catholic Church acknowledged that the Holy Spirit could teach us through the life and written works of a woman. Teresa was beatified in 1614 and canonized in 1622—her holiness was recognized not that long after her death in 1582. She made a huge impression on the Catholic landscape by founding numerous convents throughout Spain. She was friends with the man who would become St. John of the Cross, who partnered with her in reforming Carmelite communities both male and female.

These administrative activities presented Teresa as a woman of action and strong will. However, it was her understanding of the interior life—specifically, the layered region of prayer—that earned her, eventually, the title Doctor of the Church.

This book is written at a time when we have two living popes, and they are considered quite different from each other in terms of their communication styles and what, within the Catholic Church's beliefs, each has emphasized. As evidence of St. Teresa's universal appeal, I quote Pope Benedict and Pope Francis at some length.

From Pope Benedict XVI:

> Prayer is life and develops gradually, in pace with the growth of Christian life: it begins with vocal prayer, passes through interiorization by means of meditation and recollection, until it attains the union of love with Christ and with the Holy Trinity. Obviously, in the development of prayer climbing to the highest steps does not mean abandoning the previous type of prayer. Rather, it is a gradual deepening of the relationship with God that envelops the whole of life.
>
> Rather than a pedagogy, Teresa's is a true "mystagogy" of prayer: she teaches those who read her works how to pray by praying with them. Indeed, she often interrupts her account or exposition with a prayerful outburst.
>
> Another subject dear to the Saint is the centrality of Christ's humanity. For Teresa, in fact, Christian life is the personal relationship with Jesus that culminates in union with him through grace, love and imitation. Hence the importance she attaches to meditation on the Passion and on the Eucharist as the presence of Christ in the Church for the life of every believer, and as the heart of the Liturgy. St Teresa lives out unconditional love for the Church: she shows a lively *"sensus Ecclesiae,"* in the face of the episodes of division and conflict in the Church of her time.
>
> ... Dear brothers and sisters, St. Teresa of Jesus is a true teacher of Christian life for the faithful of every time. In our society, which all too often lacks spiritual values, St. Teresa teaches us to be unflagging witnesses of God, of his presence and of his action. She teaches us truly to feel this thirst for God that exists in the depths of our hearts, this desire to see God, to seek God, to be in conversation with him and to be his friends.
>
> This is the friendship we all need that we must seek anew, day after day. May the example of this Saint, profoundly contemplative and effectively active, spur us too every day to dedicate the right time to prayer, to this openness to God, to

this journey, in order to seek God, to see him, to discover his friendship and so to find true life; . . .

Therefore time devoted to prayer is not time wasted, it is time in which the path of life unfolds, the path unfolds to learning from God an ardent love for him, for his Church, and practical charity for our brothers and sisters. Many thanks.[2]

And from Pope Francis:

St. Teresa is above all a *teacher of prayer*. The discovery of the humanity of Christ was central to her experience. Moved by the desire to share this personal experience with others, she describes it in a lively and simple manner, within the reach of all, for it consists simply in "being on terms of friendship . . . with Him who, we know, loves us" (*Vida*, 8, 5). Often the narrative itself transforms into a prayer, as if she wished to introduce the reader to her inner dialogue with Christ. Teresa's prayer was not reserved to only one space or one moment of the day; it arose spontaneously on many different occasions: "It would be hard if our prayers could only be made in corners" (*The Book of the Foundations*, v, p. 31). She was certain of the value of constant, albeit not always perfect prayer. The Saint asks us to be persevering, faithful, even in the midst of aridity, of personal difficulties or of the pressing needs that call to us.

In order to renew consecrated life today, Teresa left us a great treasure, full of practical suggestions, ways and methods to pray, which, far from closing us within ourselves or leading us only to achieve interior balance, enable us to always set out again from Jesus and constitute an authentic school to grow in love of God and neighbour.[3]

Teresa's teaching on prayer becomes a theology of what it means to be a human in relationship with God. A relationship exists because two entities connect by mutual intention and action. Without God's initiation of love, there would be no relationship. Without the person's response to that love, the relationship would be incomplete, would never truly develop. Teresa recognized that the relationship we call prayer is possible only because God desires communion with us. Her writings are frequently punctuated by awe-filled gratitude for God's open arms toward us. But she also understood that God would never force us to respond or engage. Some human intention and effort are involved, after all. Of course, God provides the grace for the entire transaction.

Teresa's focus, then, was to describe what she understood to be her part of the relationship. Perhaps because she had always struggled to pray—and for a long time simply gave up praying—she learned to pay closer attention to what was going on inside her during the various practices of prayer. How did emotions help or hinder? What about those ever-present distracting thoughts? Where did the body and all its demands figure in? And what about the devil's wiles?

Also, when was it time to be concerned about a feeling or thought—and when was it better to not focus on or worry about it? When was interior work truly spiritual progress and when was it a form of self-obsession? As scholar Elizabeth A. Dreyer puts it so well, "Part of Teresa's genius was to sort out the confusion between self-knowledge and self-preoccupation and marvel that, in spite of human weakness, God dwells within, calling the desiring soul to imitate love."[4]

On the one hand, Teresa pushed and reformed until there were Carmelite convents and monasteries adhering to a more austere and demanding life in which the sisters and brothers prayed more often and lived more simply. On the other hand, she invited and urged those same brothers and sisters to trust God's ceaseless and abundant love to work with each person according to that person's gifts, calling, strengths, and weaknesses.

What we can gain from spending time with St. Teresa is a sharpened sense of everyday holiness, refined by reasonable discipline and tempered by a reawakened sensitivity to God's merciful love.

Get Ready

Here are some suggestions to prepare for your week of prayer with St. Teresa.

○ Go online to do some research of your own on Teresa of Ávila. For instance, this eleven-minute video gives a nice summary of her life: "Saint Teresa of Ávila | A Life of Mystical Experience | Carmelite Saint," September 22, 2020, YouTube video, 11:01, https://www.youtube.com/watch?v=0ui1WtoAX7o.

○ Compose three or four questions about your own life of prayer. You can refer to these questions throughout the week as you read and pray.

Week 2, Sunday

PREPARATION

What do you find intriguing about St. Teresa of Ávila so far? What do you hope to learn from her?

Read the following gospel passage several times, noting words or phrases that stand out for you. Try to summarize in your own words what Jesus is doing. Imagine your reactions to him as if you were one of those traveling and ministering along with him.

Gospel for the Week:
Matthew 6:5–13, NRSVCE

"And whenever you pray, do not be like the hypocrites; for they love to stand and pray in the synagogues and at the street corners, so that they may be seen by others. Truly I tell you, they have received their reward. But whenever you pray, go into your room and shut the door and pray to your Father who is in secret; and your Father who sees in secret will reward you.

"When you are praying, do not heap up empty phrases as the Gentiles do; for they think that they will be heard because of their many words. Do not be like them, for your Father knows what you need before you ask him.

"Pray then in this way:

> Our Father in heaven,
>> hallowed be your name.
> Your kingdom come.
> Your will be done,
>> on earth as it is in heaven.
> Give us this day our daily bread.
> And forgive us our debts,
>> as we also have forgiven our debtors.
> And do not bring us to the time of trial,
>> but rescue us from the evil one."

Identify various characteristics of your prayer experiences. In what ways do you struggle with prayer? What has helped you pray? Do you pray more easily when you're with other people or when you're alone? What prayer practices have worked best for you, and why do you think this is so?

Inspiration from St. Teresa

Here's what a friendship with our dearest Companion, our holiest God, is like. In it, intimacy is always possible and can't be stopped, except on our side, for God is always open to us. Nothing can come between us and God, our Spouse, and we can be alone with God whenever we want, as long as we want. All we must do is desire it.

So let us close the door on our worldly calendars and deadlines and live instead in paradise with the God of love. If we desire this closeness that comes from closing the door on the world, we must realize that that door is our hearts. We don't have to be mystics to accomplish this communion. We only need to focus on God with our will. That's all. It's our own choice, and because God loves us, we can do this.

Don't confuse this state with empty silence. I am speaking of a turning inward and a listening.[5]

Prayer for the Week

God, my creator, continue to create your life in me. Jesus, my Savior and brother, continue to lead the way. Holy Spirit, my helper, continue to form holy wonders in my life. Amen.

Week 2, Monday

ACKNOWLEDGING THAT GOD DWELLS IN US

Morning Prayer

Scripture: 1 Corinthians 6:19

> Do you not know that your body is a temple of the Holy Spirit within you, which you have from God, and that you are not your own?

The work for which Teresa is probably best known is *The Interior Castle*, whereby she describes the human soul in which the person encounters God—through a series of deeper and deeper chambers representing an ever more intimate connection with God. It is not easy reading, but the concept of the soul as a dwelling place for the Divine is beneficial even if we perceive ourselves functioning in one of the more exterior and less intimate rooms. I believe that one of Teresa's greatest gifts to us is her certainty of God's action within us. She had personal experience of every level of communion with God in her interior castle, yet her focus—at least with her readers—was the joy each of us can know simply because God has chosen to reside in us. The various levels of dwelling are revealed to people as they are called and as God wills, but the fact of God's presence in the human soul is constant.

From St. Teresa

> I thought of the soul as resembling a castle, formed of a single diamond or a very transparent crystal, and containing many rooms, just as in heaven there are many mansions. If we reflect, sisters, we shall see that the soul of the just man is but a paradise, in which, God tells us, He takes His delight [Proverbs 8:31]. What, do you imagine, must that dwelling be in which a King so mighty, so wise, and so pure, containing in Himself all good, can delight to rest? Nothing can

be compared to the great beauty and capabilities of a soul; however keen our intellects may be, they are as unable to comprehend them as to comprehend God, for, as He has told us, He created us in His own image and likeness.

As this is so, we need not tire ourselves by trying to realize all the beauty of this castle, although, being His creature, there is all the difference between the soul and God that there is between the creature and the Creator; the fact that it is made in God's image teaches us how great are its dignity and loveliness. It is no small misfortune and disgrace that, through our own fault, we neither understand our nature nor our origin.[6]

Unless we want to be blind and foolish, and if we have faith, it is clear that he is within us. Why, then, do we need to go and seek him a long way off? We know that the good Jesus is with us until we have consumed the accidents of bread with our natural energy. How can we doubt that he will work miracles when he is within us, if we have faith? How can we doubt that he will give us what we ask of him since he is in our house?[7]

Ask Some Questions

1. When I pray, where am I locating God in my imagination?
    Is God "up there" and outside of me?
    Can I picture myself meeting God within my own soul?
    If so, what does that look like?

2. St. Teresa asks, "What, do you imagine, must that dwelling be in which
    a King so mighty, so wise, and so pure, containing in Himself all good,
    can delight to rest?" How would I describe my interior castle?
        If it were a physical place, what colors would it be?
        What kind of music would be playing there?
        What are the primary emotions of its atmosphere?
        Most important, how do I feel about God of the Universe walking
    into my rooms?

3. What does it mean to me that God dwells within me?
        Do I believe that this truly is the case?
        How do I perceive God's presence in my soul—or what reason do
    I have to doubt that this is so?
        When am I most likely to sense that God is with me—and when
    God is absent?

A Practice

Draw a representation of your soul as you know it while acknowledging that your understanding of yourself is incomplete and cloudy. What rooms are in your interior castle, and what happens in each of them? To which rooms are you comfortable inviting God? How do you relate to God in these various regions of your soul?

Closing Prayer

God of the Universe, I don't understand how you can be my Creator and yet dwell within my tiny, flawed life. Help me grow in my acceptance of your presence within me. When we are conversing, remind me, Holy Spirit, to think of you within my own soul's rooms. Forgive me for taking so lightly the amazing truth of your dwelling in me. Amen.

Evening Prayer

- I take a few deep, slow breaths and invite the Holy Spirit to help me pray.
- To do with my body what I hope to do with my spirit, I stand or sit up, lift my face to the sky, and open my arms. And I pray: Shower your peace, O Lord, over my tired heart at the end of this day. Help me remain still and unafraid, listening for you. Amen.

Prayer to St. Teresa

St. Teresa, may your truthful yet gentle spirit accompany me as I ponder what it means to be a dwelling place of Almighty God. You never pretended to fully understand this truth, and I certainly don't grasp it. But you have helped me see that this is an important aspect of my prayer life and the growth of my faith. I really want to become more aware of—and appreciative of—God's residing within me. Amen.

Scripture: Psalm 24:7

Lift up your heads, O gates!
and be lifted up, O ancient doors!
that the King of glory may come in.

Look for Growth

What might happen when I see myself as God's dwelling place?

- o   I perceive God as closer to me than when I thought of God "out there."
- o   I am compelled to question how hospitable my interior self is toward Almighty God.
- o   Self-loathing is no longer an option because this self contains divine love.
- o   I automatically become more reflective and interested in exploring my interior world.

Prayer from, or Inspired by, St. Teresa

O Almighty God! How profound are Thy secrets and how different are spiritual matters from anything that can be seen or heard in this world! I can find nothing to which to liken these graces, insignificant as they are compared with many

others Thou dost bestow on souls. This favour acts so strongly upon the spirit that it is consumed by desires yet knows
not what to ask, for it realizes clearly that its God is with it.
You may inquire, if it realizes this so clearly, what more does it
desire and why is it pained? What greater good can it seek?[8]

Gospel Sentence: John 16:13–14

But when he comes, the Spirit of truth, he will guide you to all truth.
He will not speak on his own, but he will speak what he hears, and
will declare to you the things that are coming. He will glorify me,
because he will take from what is mine and declare it to you.

As a retreat leader over many years, I have discovered that many Christians
are still not comfortable with the idea that God dwells within them. They
may know the scriptures about our bodies being the temple of the Holy
Spirit and about how we are in Christ and Christ and God are one and we
are all united, and so forth. Yet when the time comes that we need wisdom
or some other help from God, we tend to look outward and hope for new
information—as if God has not been building an interior castle of wisdom,
virtue, and experience in us for a long time already. Rather than ask the
Holy Spirit to remind us of what we have already learned, we wait for a
new revelation. Rather than look inward to where God resides and speaks
to us, we seek the word of a pastor or other "expert."

This becomes a failure of spiritual confidence, and it costs us much
peace and hinders our discernment. Does the Holy Spirit dwell in us or
not? If so, why do we not trust this Advocate and Comforter to do what was
promised? Do we think ourselves humble in assuming that we don't know
enough and that we have no real wisdom? Perhaps we should consider this
not so much humility as a lack of faith in God's persistent action within us.

St. Teresa talked about the necessity of humility—a lot. But she did
not back down on the fact that God generously shows us mercy, longs for
us, and works in our souls even when we are unaware of it.

Week 2, Tuesday

CELEBRATING THE GIFTS WE HAVE

Morning Prayer

Scripture: 1 Corinthians 12:4–7

> Now there are varieties of gifts, but the same Spirit; and there are
> varieties of services, but the same Lord; and there are varieties of
> activities, but it is the same God who activates all of them in every-
> one. To each is given the manifestation of the Spirit for the common
> good.

Teresa did not seek extraordinary and sensational gifts or experiences from
God. She sought to love God, follow Jesus, purify her heart, and live out her
calling as a Carmelite nun. When she did begin to have mystical experiences, they caused as much outward trouble as inward good because it took a
long time for Teresa's superiors to recognize her bizarre outward signs as
the workings of the Holy Spirit. She suffered in this tension for many years.

Furthermore, she never supposed that deep contemplation and ecstasy were required for a full life with God. In fact, she discouraged nuns of
certain temperaments from practicing some forms of prayer because she
thought this might lead to emotional instability and spiritual problems.
Her grasp of the breadth of God's graces made a safe place for a person
to explore what God wanted for *her*, regardless of what others experienced.

In this way, Teresa was almost radical in her belief that God knew what
each soul needed and that uniformity of practices and prayer methods was,
frankly, overrated. She had faced her own struggles with modes of prayer
that simply didn't work well for her; there was a time when she claimed
she could not pray unless she used a book. This from a woman who later
met God in mystical trances and ecstasies!

Her confidence in God's intimate connection with each person expand-
ed the realm of prayer for her nuns and for so many of us in the centuries

since. God loves us passionately and completely. God will work in us whatever needs to happen; our part is to turn to God in receptivity.

From St. Teresa

Saint Martha was holy, but we are not told that she was a contemplative. What more could you want than to grow to be like her, who was worthy to receive Christ our Lord so often in her house, and to prepare meals for him, and to serve him and perhaps eat at table with him? If she had been always absorbed in devotion, as Saint Mary Magdalene was, no one would have prepared a meal for this Divine Guest. Remember that our little community [she is speaking to the nuns of her convent] is Saint Martha's house and that there are people of all kinds here. Nuns who are called to the active life must not murmur at others who are absorbed in contemplation. Contemplatives know that, although they themselves may be silent, the Lord will speak for them. As a rule, this makes them forget themselves and everything else.

Remember that there must be someone to cook the meals. Count yourselves happy in being able to serve like Martha. Remember that true humility consists in being ready for what the Lord wants to do with you and happy that he should do it, and in considering yourselves unworthy to be called his servants. If contemplation, mental and vocal prayer, tending the sick, serving in the house, and working at even the lowliest tasks serve the Guest who comes to stay with us, eat with us, and take his recreation with us, what should it matter if we do one of these things rather than another?[9]

Engage in some spiritual recreation, such as conversation (so long as it is really spiritual), or a country walk, according as your confessor advises. In all these things it is important to have had experience, for from this we learn what is fitting for us; but let God be served in all things. Sweet is His yoke, and it is essential that we should not drag the soul along with us, so to say, but lead it gently, so that it may make the greater progress.[10]

Ask Some Questions

1. What kind of prayer experiences have I sought?

    What experiences have I considered to be superior or "more mature" than others?

    And what brought me to see things this way?

    Have I sometimes tried to "drag my soul along" rather than lead it gently to discover what is best for it?

2. What is my place in this Body of Christ?

    What functions do I seem to perform most often and most naturally?

    What actions and ministries give me joy?

    And what gifts do others seek in me: what help do they ask from me, and what role do they see me playing in their lives?

3. Have I resented not receiving a spiritual gift I wanted?

     What made me value that gift and long for it?

     Or what gift or function do I have in God's work that I may have undervalued or neglected?

A Practice

Sit down for a relaxed but detailed conversation with St. Teresa and the Holy Spirit. Talk about the prayer experiences you have had and the gifts you have offered to God's kingdom. Allow time for your companions to respond to you. Ask them if they have noticed you avoiding certain kinds of prayer or activity—if you have perhaps rejected graces and gifts that have been given to you. Try to identify your feelings about these matters. Talk about your doubts or resentments, your feelings of not being good enough or not being given what you asked for. Take some notes of this conversation. Allow it to move you into prayer to Jesus and God the Father/Mother.

Closing Prayer

God, my Creator, you know the experiences I need the most, and you know which gifts are meant for me. At times I have pushed back against those things because I had my heart set on another kind of experience or another way of serving you. To be honest, I have been envious of other people because you seemed to give them a mission, gift, or experience that I wanted. Please forgive me for not trusting your wisdom in how my life and gifts have unfolded. Help me recognize the gifts and graces you have given me. Then help me receive them and give you thanks. Then show me how to engage with them for the good of your loving will for this world. Amen.

Evening Prayer

o   I take a few deep, slow breaths and invite the Holy Spirit to help me pray.

o   To do with my body what I hope to do with my spirit, I sit up (or stand), lift my face to the sky, and open my arms. And I pray: Holy Spirit, who activates holy gifts in each person, forgive me for resisting your work in my life. Thank you for the abundance of graces you have placed within me and help me receive them joyfully and with due humility. Amen.

Prayer to St. Teresa

St. Teresa, thank you for calming my anxiety about how to serve God. You remind me that God provides the gifts and desires we need to do what God wants from us. I keep striving as if everything is up to me, and I worry that I should be doing something else—a better service—or that I have missed some crucial resource that is necessary for me to please God. You assure me that God simply wants my heart, honesty, desire, and receptivity to divine generosity. Amen.

Scripture: 1 Corinthians 12:14–26

Indeed, the body does not consist of one member but of many. If the foot were to say, "Because I am not a hand, I do not belong to the body," that would not make it any less a part of the body. And if the ear would say, "Because I am not an eye, I do not belong to the body," that would not make it any less a part of the body. If the whole body were an eye, where would the hearing be? If the whole body were hearing, where would the sense of smell be? But as it is, God arranged the members in the body, each one of them, as he chose. If all were a single member, where would the body be? As it is, there are many members, yet one body. The eye cannot say to the hand, "I have no need of you," nor again the head to the feet, "I have no need of you." On the contrary, the members of the body that seem to be weaker are indispensable, and those members of the body that we think less honorable we clothe with greater honor, and our less respectable members are treated with greater respect; whereas our more respectable members do not need this. But God has so arranged the body, giving the greater honor to the inferior member, that there may be no dissension within the body, but the members may have the same care for one another. If one member suffers, all suffer together with it; if one member is honored, all rejoice together with it.

Look for Growth

What might happen when I receive whatever gifts and experiences God has given me?

o   I stop comparing myself to others.
o   God can draw me out of my self-preoccupation and into true ministry with others.
o   I can engage with my gifts more deeply and authentically.
o   The Holy Spirit can teach me contentment and joy.

Prayer from, or Inspired by, St. Teresa

O Lord, grant that my love be not the fruit of my imagination but be proved by works. What can I do for You who died for us and created us and gave us being, without counting myself fortunate in being able to repay You something of what I owe you? Well do I know, my Lord, of how little I am capable. But I shall be able to do all things provided You do not withdraw from me.[11]

Gospel Sentence: Matthew 4:19

He said to them, "Come after me, and I will make you fishers of men."

This topic of gifts and experiences in the writings of St. Teresa resonates with me because it has been an area of struggle through the years. I have tended to look with longing at others' lives and thus shortchanged the gifts and privileges in my own. It has been tempting to long after the lives of women who could have children rather than receive my childless life as fully blessed by God. Or I have envied friends who could give their full energy to writing while I fought rising resentment at having to work a "day job" for decades. And doesn't it seem that God just speaks more frequently and dramatically to other people? That their prayer lives lead to leadership positions or best-selling books?

Make no mistake: St. Teresa would have been well acquainted with envy and resentment in the context of a religious community. Nuns have the same human nature as the rest of us. Surely the sister who could meditate for hours was seen as a bit higher up in God's eyes than the one who stuck with vocal prayers and tended the garden. Or the nun with the gift for dramatic storytelling came across as always being in the midst of God's adventures, while the others worked quietly in the kitchen or scrubbed the floors and repeated the Our Father countless times without any drama whatsoever. Teresa wrote *The Way of Perfection* for the sake of her community, and she found it necessary to stress numerous times that God worked different ways in different people—and that humility was of utmost importance.

You don't have to belong to a religious community to see this tension of gifts and roles play out. Church culture has not always been helpful with this. We still pay much more attention to the talented musician or speaker than we do the person who keeps the church accounts in order. Some members of Christ's Body are indeed "less honorable" and for that reason must be treated with greater honor, but we don't always do this. It is easier to elevate some gifts and contributions and ignore others. Just as it is our tendency to call some things God's special blessings—such as a good job and a beautiful family—while acting as if the person without those things has somehow missed God's favor. Teresa knew better, and so should we.

Week 2, Wednesday

TRUSTING GOD'S WORK IN US

Morning Prayer

Scripture: Ephesians 2:8–10

For by grace you have been saved through faith, and this is not your own doing; it is the gift of God—not the result of works, so that no one may boast. For we are what he has made us, created in Christ Jesus for good works, which God prepared beforehand to be our way of life.

Teresa entered the Carmelite order as one who, for quite some time, had not considered herself convent material. She like to be liked, and she enjoyed her social life. As she grew in awareness in her life as a nun, she recognized just how much she had compromised her soul because of her tendency to be influenced by others, especially friends who did not especially encourage a virtuous life but were more likely to waste her time and energy in foolish conversation and distractions.

At least she was able and willing to see herself honestly, and this made it possible for her to see God's work within her. She did not presume that she was virtuous enough or spiritually accomplished enough to receive graces and grow in true devotion. Her frank self-assessment threw light on just how merciful God was with her and just how much initiation God took with a human person. In fact, God did not expect from Teresa what she could not accomplish by will or intention.

In her exploration of the interior castle—the various levels within the soul whereby the person grows in union with God—Teresa identified the more intimate levels as those at which the person exercises less and less consciousness and direct action. Thus the mystical experience is one in which we let go of ourselves and receive whatever God has prepared for us. God creates the encounter; our part is to desire God and remain receptive. Receptivity is not the same as passivity. We grow in union with God not by sitting by complacently but by desiring God expectantly. The desire does not cause the act of communion but opens the soul so that God's loving action can be received.

From St. Teresa

I have often reflected with amazement upon God's great goodness and my soul has delighted in the thought of His great magnificence and mercy. May He be blessed for all this for it has become clear to me that, even in this life, He has not failed to reward me for any of my good desires. However wretched and imperfect my good works have been, this Lord of mine has been improving them, perfecting them and making them of greater worth, and yet hiding my evil deeds and my sins as soon as they have been committed. He has even allowed the eyes of those who have seen them to be blind to them and He blots them from their memory. He gilds my faults and makes some virtue of mine to shine forth in splendour; yet it was He Himself Who gave it me and almost forced me to possess it.[12]

I repeat my advice, then (and it matters not how often I say this, for it is of great importance), that one must never be depressed or afflicted because of aridities or unrest or distraction of the mind. If a person would gain spiritual freedom and not be continually troubled, let him begin by not being afraid of the Cross and he will find that the Lord will help him to bear it; he will then advance happily and find profit in everything. It is now clear that, if no water is coming from the well, we ourselves can put none into it. But of course we must not be careless: water must always be drawn when there is any there, for at such a time God's will is that we should use it so that He may multiply our virtues.[13]

Ask Some Questions

1. In looking back over my spiritual history, how much importance have
    I placed on personal effort when it came to growing in faith or virtue?
        Have I ever felt weary from trying to grow or become more like
    Christ?

2. St. Teresa stresses that a person should "never be depressed or afflicted
    because of aridities or unrest or distraction of the mind." What do I
    make of this?
        How can I balance "spiritual freedom . . . not be continually trou-
    bled" with taking some responsibility for my life with God?

3. How might my life be different if I stopped worrying about my spiritual
    state and instead turned to God with an open heart every day, expecting
    God's grace to make everything work?

A Practice

Make a list of your spiritual shortcomings. Be brief if honest.

Bring this list to prayer. Talk about the items, one by one, with Jesus, who—remember—was fully human and who traveled, ministered, and lived with a group of very human disciples. Your shortcomings are neither shocking nor surprising to Jesus. Try to listen to Jesus' response to your "confession list."

Ponder Philippians 2:12–13. In the first Bible version cited below, we see a significant tension between our effort and God's work in us:

> Therefore, my beloved, just as you have always obeyed me, not only in my presence, but much more now in my absence, work out your own salvation with fear and trembling; for it is God who is at work in you, enabling you both to will and to work for his good pleasure.

For a slightly different take on this, consider this passage in Eugene Peterson's paraphrase, *The Message*:

> What I'm getting at, friends, is that you should simply keep on doing what you've done from the beginning. When I was living among you, you lived in responsive obedience. Now that I'm separated from you, keep it up. Better yet, redouble your efforts. Be energetic in your life of salvation, reverent and sensitive before God. That energy is *God's* energy, an energy deep within you, God himself willing and working at what will give him the most pleasure.

Write down your response to these verses. Perhaps turn your response into a prayer.

Closing Prayer

Lord God, it's such a mystery to me how all of this works. I want to "work out my salvation"—cultivate my relationship with you with true effort and intention. I also want to let go and allow you to do the transformative work in me. Teach me how to do this. Amen.

Evening Prayer

o   I take a few deep, slow breaths and invite the Holy Spirit to help me pray.
o   To do with my body what I hope to do with my spirit, I sit up (or stand), lift my face to the sky, and open my arms. And I pray: May I rest in the security of your infinite love, O Lord. May I count on your faithfulness. May I turn fully to you. May I receive whatever gifts, tasks, graces, and understandings you desire for me. Amen.

Prayer to St. Teresa

Dear St. Teresa, please stay by my side as I try to trust God more. Amen.

Scripture: Ephesians 2:4–7

But God, who is rich in mercy, out of the great love with which he loved us even when we were dead through our trespasses, made us alive together with Christ—by grace you have been saved—and raised us up with him and seated us with him in the heavenly places in Christ Jesus, so that in the ages to come he might show the immeasurable riches of his grace in kindness toward us in Christ Jesus.

Look for Growth

What might happen when I trust God to do the transformative work in my soul?

- o I focus on God, not on myself.
- o My faith is encouraged to grow as I expect God to meet me and work in me.
- o I put away doubt, self-loathing, shame, and regret.
- o I take on a posture of openness and expectation, allowing God to reach me.

Prayer from, or Inspired by, St. Teresa

O infinite goodness of my God! It is thus that I seem to see both myself and Thee. O Joy of the angels, how I long, when I think of this, to be wholly consumed in love for Thee! How true it is that Thou dost bear with those who cannot bear Thee to be with them! Oh, how good a Friend art Thou, my Lord! How Thou dost comfort us and suffer us and wait until our nature becomes more like Thine and meanwhile dost bear with it as it is! Thou dost remember the times when we love Thee, my Lord, and, when for a moment we repent, Thou dost forget how we have offended Thee. I have seen this clearly in my own life, and I cannot conceive, my Creator, why the whole world does not strive to draw near to Thee in this intimate friendship.[14]

Gospel Sentence: Matthew 11:30

For my yoke is easy, and my burden light.

There was a time when I dove into a depression out of sheer spiritual exhaustion. I know I am not alone in this. So many of us grow up with that wonderful American work ethic as well as the idea that an individual can determine their own fate with enough grit, independence, and hard work. These factors can really work against the faith-filled mindset of depending completely on divine love and grace. St. Teresa and so many of our saints understood that every breath we take is a gift, that God's love for creation is the energy that keeps the universe in motion. Not only that—and this is truly mind-boggling—but God's love is the energy that works upon every molecule of the human person, from head to toe and from sense to soul.

Teresa's acceptance of this mystery freed her to be herself with God, to work hard at prayer, compassion, and the endurance of suffering, but at the same time trust God to do the heavy lifting. She knew that everything about her—from her mixed motives to her not-quite-humility when under duress—was flawed. And yet she was joyful! She had discovered that God's love transcended all the incompletion, shortfalls, and thwarted efforts.

The truth is, our spiritual exhaustion is often the logical outcome of works without faith. We try and try to pray more, act better, and speak kindlier. We cling to our own efforts when we could let go of ourselves, our hoped-for outcome, our longing after "spiritual success." Yes, it's possible for spiritual effort to become a vehicle for pride. I'm sure this is one reason Teresa talked so much of humility. She knew that people cannot grasp after success—even spiritual success—without imparting to themselves undue importance and power.

Are you weary in your soul? Have you grown dispirited and cynical about this entire spiritual endeavor? Perhaps you can sit with Jesus and ask him something like this: Lord, you said that your yoke is easy and your burden light, but my yoke is hard and my burden heavy. Show me how truly I can come to you and learn from you. Help me let you do the heavy lifting.

Week 2, Thursday

FINDING GOOD COMPANIONS

Morning Prayer

Scripture: 1 Thessalonians 5:13–15

Be at peace among yourselves. And we urge you, beloved, to admonish the idlers, encourage the fainthearted, help the weak, be patient with all of them. See that none of you repays evil for evil, but always seek to do good to one another and to all.

We think of St. Teresa as a true individual, one who claimed her life in Christ as the unique expression it was. She blazed trails in the exploration of spirituality and held fast to the truth God revealed to her personally, even when others misunderstood her and suspected her experiences of falling outside the realm of God's action. Perhaps the long years of suffering such questions and rejection increased her sensitivity to the need for fellowship and mutual support within the community of faith.

Keep in mind that Teresa made strict reforms in the Carmelite order. When she joined it, life in the cloister had become lax in prayer and too accustomed to entertaining company in the parlor. Teresa worked for years to bring the community to a sharper and more constant focus upon their calling of prayer and holy work, eventually forming a new branch, the Discalced Carmelites, who would maintain higher standards. She established many convents throughout Spain.

Yet Teresa placed great importance on the communal aspects of life in a convent. She wrote *The Way of Perfection* to help the sisters discern God's way in their life together and as individuals. And she greatly valued the role of a confessor in her life—the priest who heard her confessions and counseled her—even though it was years before she found one who helped her accept her mystical experiences as from God. Until then, she had struggled to be truthful with whatever priest she met with; most distrusted her mystical episodes, some to the point of believing them demonic. When at last she sat with a wise man who recognized God's working in her, she knew what a gift she had been given.

It is no surprise, then, that the saint warned against attempting the journey of faith alone. She recognized the crucial need for companionship and the necessity of the right kind of companion—one with whom a person could honestly share their struggles and joys in their life of prayer, work, community, and relationship with God.

From St. Teresa

It is a great evil for a soul beset by so many dangers to be alone. I believe, if I had had anyone with whom to discuss all this, it would have helped me not to fall again, if only because I should have been ashamed in his sight, which I was not in the sight of God. For this reason I would advise those who practice prayer, especially at first, to cultivate friendship and intercourse with others of similar interests. This is a most important thing, if only because we can help each other by our prayers, and it is all the more so because it may bring us many other benefits. Since people can find comfort in the conversation and human sympathy of ordinary friendships, even when these are not altogether good, I do not know why anyone who is beginning to love and serve God in earnest should not be allowed to discuss his joys and trials with others—and people who practice prayer have plenty of both. For, if the friendship which such a person desires to have with His Majesty is true friendship, he need not be afraid of becoming vainglorious: as soon as the first motion of vainglory attacks him, he will repel it, and, in doing so, gain merit. I believe that anyone who discusses the subject with this in mind will profit both himself and his hearers, and will be all the wiser for it; and, without realizing he is doing so, will edify his friends.[15]

It is of the utmost importance for the beginner to associate with those who lead a spiritual life, and not only with those in the same mansion as herself, but with others who have travelled farther into the castle, who will aid her greatly and draw her to join them.[16]

Ask Some Questions

1. Who have been my companions in the faith?

    When have I (a) benefited from the right spiritual friend at the right time, or (b) suffered because I had no friend to accompany me spiritually?

2. How important is it to me to talk about my faith journey with another? What attracts me to this kind of sharing, or what repels me from it?

3. Recall these phrases from 1 Thessalonians above: "Admonish the idlers, encourage the fainthearted, help the weak, be patient with all." Who, if anyone, has permission to admonish me—that is, speak up when they see me heading toward trouble? (We can assume that admonishing could be applied to situations other than idleness.)

    Is there anyone for whom I have been that voice of caution?

    Do I see much healthy admonishing going on among the Christians I know?

    If so, what makes it helpful and effective?

    If not, why might people be avoiding this aspect of spiritual companionship?

A Practice

Finish these sentences:

o   I need spiritual companionship most when . . .

o   Sometimes, it's better for me to be alone, such as when . . .

o   A person who is a good spiritual companion for me is . . .

o   I don't really have this kind of friend right now, but I wonder if [name] would be willing to meet me for coffee and talk about the faith journey.

Closing Prayer

Holy Trinity, you demonstrate for us unity and true fellowship among Father, Son, and Holy Spirit. Help me and others in my faith community learn more about how to be good spiritual companions to one another. Amen.

Evening Prayer

o   I take a few deep, slow breaths and invite the Holy Spirit to help me pray.

o   To do with my body what I hope to do with my spirit, I sit up (or stand), lift my face to the sky, and open my arms. And I pray: Thank you, Heavenly Father, for the human relationships you have blessed me with. Thank you, Lord Jesus, for modeling friendship through your compassion, truth telling, instruction, and infinite patience. Thank you, Holy Spirit, for your constant work of building and nurturing the Body of Christ. Amen.

Prayer to St. Teresa

St. Teresa, you learned the importance of true community that is formed from love and humility. So often, "community" in my world is a treacherous place where competition and gossip threaten peace. You didn't have social media, but I'm sure you understand the temptations I face and the loneliness I feel sometimes. Keep pointing me to Jesus. Amen.

Scripture: Galatians 6:1–2

My friends, if anyone is detected in a transgression, you who have received the Spirit should restore such a one in a spirit of gentleness. Take care that you yourselves are not tempted. Bear one another's burdens, and in this way you will fulfill the law of Christ.

Look for Growth

What might happen when I seek and nurture edifying spiritual friendship?

o   I grow in sensitivity to what another person is going through.
o   I develop the habit of prayerfulness in my human friendships.
o   God is able to help me through other people.
o   Christ's Body is built up and strengthened right where I am.

Prayer from, or Inspired by, St. Teresa

St. Teresa, you know how the soul longs to be known, understood, received, and loved—primarily, by our dear Lord Jesus, but also by fellow pilgrims on the way. Please help me become a true companion to others. And with the Lord's help, send me the spiritual friends I need. Amen.

Gospel Sentence: John 13:34

As I have loved you, so you also should love one another.

Friendship of any kind can get complicated, messy, and painful. When I know another person and that person knows me—the real me—it's inevitable that my less-than-lovely facets will be discovered. Honesty brings out my truest, holiest gifts but also my unfinished virtues and unhealed wounds. This is true of a friendship that does not necessarily have a spiritual focus.

Add to an honest friendship the intentional discussion of spirituality and we tap a deeper, even more complex realm of information and emotion. The spiritual companion not only listens to my words but also listens for God's voice in the conversation. A spiritual friend assumes that Another is always present when concerns are shared, laughter breaks out, or tears spill. A spiritual friend seeks to express the compassion and wisdom of Christ and does not shy away from the needed question or the challenge to stretch a little, try something new, or face a difficult truth.

Spiritual friendship is a tall order, and it's not always easy to find. For some of us, a spiritual director fills that need for a companion on the journey. This relationship is not friendship in the typical sense, but it provides a safe place in which to talk about the gutsy work of prayer, discernment, forgiveness, grief, and so on. A good spiritual director helps me see myself better and directs me consistently to God's mercy and invitation.

For those of us who become spiritual directors, the process of companioning becomes a graced place of witness. What a joy to affirm in another the courage I see in them or the growth in their faith. What a privilege to receive that person's story as the sacred Good News that it is. I may serve in the capacity of spiritual companion, but that service becomes a certain kind of portal into God's kingdom—the portal of a single life longing for the Divine.

Teresa of Ávila knew firsthand that the spiritual journey toward holiness, spiritual freedom, and real love is sometimes a treacherous and lonely path. She treasured the people in whom she could confide about her interior travels. If such a strong and impressive woman recognized her need for good friends in the faith, then the rest of us can seek such company without apology. We need a helping hand and a listening ear. And we can become those things for someone else.

Week 2, Friday

TURNING OUR EYES
UPON JESUS

Morning Prayer

Scripture: Isaiah 26:3, NKJV

You will keep *him* in perfect peace,
Whose mind *is* stayed on *You*,
Because he trusts in You.

In Teresa of Ávila we find a woman who had learned to trust her personal experience of God, to the point of continuing her prayers and devotion when others thought her experiences were not legitimately from God. Through years of this tension, Teresa continued to meet with God, fix her eyes upon Christ, and be true to what she discovered in those experiences. We can honestly say that she was unafraid to be an individual in communion with God.

Yet how did she maintain this risky sort of spiritual independence without drifting into error or out of communion with her religious community? She kept her gaze upon God. Hers was not a self-focused or navel-gazing independence of soul. She could be brave and, in some ways, survive apart from certain social supports because her faith was fixed and founded upon the Source of all her wisdom and spiritual energy.

From St. Teresa

I am not asking you to become involved in long and subtle meditations with your understanding and reason. I am only asking you to look at him. Who can prevent you from turning the eyes of your soul upon this Lord? You can look at very ugly things; can't you, then, look at the most beautiful thing imaginable? Your Spouse never takes his eyes off you. He has endured patiently thousands of foul and abominable sins you have committed against him, yet even your sins have not been enough to make him turn his eyes away from you. Is it so hard for you to look away from outward things sometimes and to look at him? He is only waiting for us to look at him. If you want him, you will find him. He yearns so much for us to look at him that it will not be a lack of effort on his part if we fail to do so.[17]

Our understanding and will become more noble and capable of good in every way when we turn from ourselves to God: it is very injurious never to raise our minds above the mire of our own faults. . . . [W]hile we are continually absorbed in contemplating the weakness of our earthly nature, the springs of our actions will never flow free from the mire of timid, weak, and cowardly thoughts, such as: 'I wonder whether people are noticing me or not! If I follow this course, will harm come to me? Dare I begin this work?' . . . Therefore I maintain, my daughters, that we should fix our eyes on Christ our only good, and on His saints; there we shall learn true humility, and our minds will be ennobled, so that self-knowledge will not make us base and cowardly.[18]

Ask Some Questions

1. What is my experience of "looking upon" Jesus?
    How has that happened for me?
    Am I doing this consistently as part of my prayer?

2. In what ways do I become mired in my own thoughts and worries about my sins, failings, and other concerns?
    When am I most tempted to focus on my flaws?
    If I am not looking to Jesus for my strength and sustenance, then to whom or what do I turn for those things?

3. When I think of Jesus looking at me, how does that make me feel? What is my reaction to Jesus' gaze resting on me?

A Practice

Several times today, pause and allow God's gaze to rest upon you. Sit in a quiet place and open yourself to God's loving gaze. Or stand in a busy place and remind yourself that even in all the hubbub, that holy, merciful gaze is fixed upon you. When you are feeling energized, imagine God's eyes on you. When you're at a low point, invite the holy gaze. Notice how being conscious of God's gaze influences your emotions, outlook, and actions. Note what is difficult about this prayer practice. Talk to God about how you feel when being gazed upon so intently.

Closing Prayer

Lord Jesus, I don't know all the reasons I avoid looking right at you and focusing on you. Maybe I'm afraid that you'll judge me or be disappointed in me, and so I don't want our eyes to meet. Maybe I really do care about a lot of other things more than this relationship with you. And if I don't care enough, why is that? What gets between us? I know it's not anything to do with you, that you continuously invite me into conversation and your presence. I believe that you desire me and seek me out. Why don't I desire you more? Why don't I seek you more earnestly? Help me with this, please, because I cannot help myself. Amen.

Evening Prayer

○   I take a few deep, slow breaths and invite the Holy Spirit to help me pray.

○   To do with my body what I hope to do with my spirit, I sit up (or stand), lift my face to the sky, and open my arms. And I pray: Holy God, I believe that your love is always focused upon me. Help me receive it. Then, help me return it. Amen.

Prayer to St. Teresa

St. Teresa, you were so familiar with all the ways our human nature gets in the way of a clear and open friendship with God. Please accompany me as I search my heart and refocus my love on the One who loves me, gives me life, and holds a blessed future before me. Amen.

Scripture: Hebrews 12:1-3, PHILLIPS

Surrounded then as we are by these serried ranks of witnesses, let us strip off everything that hinders us, as well as the sin which dogs our feet, and let us run the race that we have to run with patience, our eyes fixed on Jesus the source and the goal of our faith. For he himself endured a cross and thought nothing of its shame because of the joy he knew would follow his suffering; and he is now seated at the right hand of God's throne. Think constantly of him enduring all that sinful men could say against him and you will not lose your purpose or your courage.

Look for Growth

What might happen when I focus on Jesus?

○   My view automatically expands, bringing more information and enlightenment.

o   My sins and struggles diminish in light of Christ's majestic presence.
o   I put myself in a better position to learn from Jesus and take my cues from him.
o   In focusing on Jesus, I become more like him.

Prayer from, or Inspired by, St. Teresa

Dear Jesus, you only want us to look at you. Forgive me for resisting this—I'm not even sure why I resist. Why does my gaze flit here and there but not to you? Thank you for looking at me even when I ignore your love. May I be drawn more and more to your beautiful gaze. Amen.

Gospel Sentence: John 15:5

I am the vine, you are the branches. Whoever remains in me and I in him will bear much fruit, because without me you can do nothing.

The focus of my energy determines the direction of my life. Energy that is directed at the self usually stirs up the self and adds to the confusion. When I become my own reference point, I don't really go anywhere beyond myself but remain in a self-fulfilling circular pattern of striving and failing. St. Teresa undoubtedly saw this happen with women in religious communities—women who truly wanted to be good nuns but who focused too much on their own efforts at holiness. This is a common pitfall for people who aspire to spiritual maturity. A person who takes seriously the whole idea of a spiritual life is primed for turning that seriousness inward. For this reason, the mentoring and discipline of spiritual leaders, such as the abbess of a convent, is paramount. A wise abbess or abbot can detect when a person is so concerned about doing the right thing spiritually that she or he becomes obsessive over rules or hypersensitive to sin—what is called scrupulosity.

Our tendency to focus too much on the self is yet another good argument for pastoral counseling and spiritual direction. Sometimes it takes another person to point out that I am assuming an inordinate amount of power in my relationship with God—I actually believe that perhaps this time I've worn out God's patience! Or that I have come up with a sin or failing that God simply cannot overcome or overlook.

Have you noticed how a parent will sometimes stop a child's activity and say, "Look at me"? The parent knows that this little one is spinning into emotional overload or trying to avoid a conversation. When the child looks into the parent's eyes, the parent is looking into the child's eyes too. And the parent's eyes are communicating calm, love, and safety. All the child needs to do is meet that gaze and the connection is made. Even if the child looks away, when she or he dares to look at Mom again, nothing has changed. Mom's eyes can bring stability to the day in just a moment or two.

Jesus is already looking at us—constantly, passionately, lovingly. As Teresa mentioned, we look at so many other things, many of them unpleasant. Why can't we train our gaze upon God? The holy gaze will bring stability to the moment. God's gaze will bring peace and perspective. That gaze will remind me that everything is not up to me.

And God's eyes will hold us steady when the day is bleak, when we are weak, when our minds get foggy, when depression lurks. We can learn to fix our eyes upon Jesus, and in doing so, we will more readily let go of our regrets and worries because we've directed our energy elsewhere—to Jesus' example, to God's promises.

Teresa's Fire

St. Teresa's lifelong study of the interior life opened for religious and laypeople alike a wonderful frontier for spiritual development. Long before the science we call psychology, she dared to explore what happens within a person that can hurt or help—in relationships with others, in the maturing of faith, in the development of a healthy and meaningful life. Her fire of understanding still helps people burn away the shame, pride, and fear that can come between us and our loving God.

In what ways have you explored your own interior life? Where has God's presence manifested in your emotions, memories, thoughts, intuitions, dreams, desires, and silences? From your experiences in the interior castle, how can you encourage others to look within and trust God to meet them there? True freedom happens inside us when we learn to commune with God in the deep places of the heart. May you find this freedom yourself and inspire others to do the same.

ST. CATHERINE OF SIENA, WHO SETS AN EXAMPLE OF SPIRITUAL POWER IN GOD'S LOVING SERVICE

> No virtue can have life in it except from charity, and charity is nursed and mothered by humility. You will find humility in the knowledge of yourself when you see that even your own existence comes not from yourself but from me, for I loved you before you came into being. And in my unspeakable love for you I willed to create you anew in grace.
>
> — *The Dialogue*[1]

I like to think of St. Catherine as the preacher for the Great Reality. Through her every relationship and communication, she expressed the bedrock truth of who we are: created by God and recipients of unrelenting and unlimited love. The closer a person draws to God, the more that love will determine their every thought, word, and deed. Catherine was tough when it came to truth, but that toughness was tempered by the love this truth had revealed to her.

Week 3, Saturday

WHO WAS CATHERINE OF SIENA?

Born to a very large family in Siena in 1347, Catherine had her first vision at age six, when she saw Jesus "in papal robes, sitting on a throne above the local Dominican church and surrounded by saints; he smiled and blessed her, but said nothing."[2] Later, when her parents wanted her to marry, she cut her hair to put off suitors and ended up for a time in a cloistered existence there at home, practicing prayers, fasting, and penance. Eventually she became involved in the Mantellate, a local community made up mainly of widows who were members of the Dominican Third Order, becoming a member in 1365. It's important to note that, as a Third Order Dominican, Catherine was not a fully vowed religious; rather, she spent her life out in the world, serving needs in the community. She wore the Dominican habit and continued to live at home, though there she was occupied with her religious practices.

People were drawn to Catherine through her work in the community nursing the sick and ministering to the poor. She was uneducated but became a teacher of faith and practice, even helping others understand the scriptures. She had grown up around Dominican and other Church influences, absorbing the theology preached and taught at the time, but what energized her teaching—and all her ministry, in fact—was her life of prayer, which often took her into mystical space where she encountered the love and mercy of God.

Along with God's love was the truth—the holy reality that became apparent to Catherine during her prayers and ecstasies. This truth would not let her go, and she was compelled to teach it, speak out for it, and fight for it.

> Her absolute refusal to compromise Truth as she experienced it in God, the urgency she felt to reverse every falsification she saw, made her look the naïve fool more than once. . . . She was indeed a social mystic—but even more properly a mystic activist. Poverty, sickness, the suffering of injustice even to the

point of death, were not merely evils or even systemic evils to
her: They were that, and as such she fought them—but they
were still more pawns in the hand of the will of *both* oppressed
and oppressor under God.[3]

This fervor for the truth—and others' recognition of her wisdom, holiness,
and gifts—brought Catherine into the political realm various times. She
became a peacemaker, the woman who scolded popes and rulers alike. Even
in a man's world, when Catherine spoke, people listened.

> When the fame of her holiness spread, she became the
> protagonist of an intense activity of spiritual guidance for
> people from every walk of life: nobles and politicians, artists
> and ordinary people, consecrated men and women and reli-
> gious, including Pope Gregory XI who was living at Avignon
> in that period and whom she energetically and effectively
> urged to return to Rome.
>
> She travelled widely to press for the internal reform of the
> Church and to foster peace among the States. It was also for
> this reason that Venerable Pope John Paul II chose to declare
> her Co-Patroness of Europe: may the Old Continent never
> forget the Christian roots that are at the origin of its progress
> and continue to draw from the Gospel the fundamental values
> that assure justice and harmony.[4]

Catherine was canonized in 1461 by Pope Pius II; she was declared a
Doctor of the Church in 1970 by Pope Paul VI; in 1999, Pope John Paul
II named her one of the patron saints of Europe. Catherine was the first
layperson to be made a Doctor of the Church.

> The Holy Father noted that, although Catherine was unable
> to read or write, this "courageous young woman" did not
> hesitate to appeal to civil and religious leaders. She called
> them to action and at times even rebuked them. Pope Francis
> mentioned in particular her work to bring peace to Italy, and
> to call for the Pope's return to Rome from Avignon.
>
> "May her example help everyone understand how to
> be united, with Christian consistency, an intense love for the
> Church with an effective solicitude for the civil community,
> especially in this time of trial," the Pope said. "I ask St Cath-
> erine to protect Italy during this pandemic, and to protect

Europe, because she is the Patroness of Europe; to protect the whole of Europe so that it may remain united."[5]

In St. Catherine we find an intriguing blend of robust activity within and without. We can be encouraged in our acquaintance with a saint who was also a layperson. God makes room in each life for the graces needed to produce wondrous fruit.

Get Ready

Here are some suggestions to prepare for the week:

○ Go online to do some research of your own on Catherine of Siena. For instance, "St. Catherine of Siena HD," November 21, 2018, YouTube video, 2:58, https://www.youtube.com/watch?v=PbGft4ARjdY; "Biography of St. Catherine of Siena," October 13, 2020, YouTube video, 12:22, https://www.youtube.com/watch?v=ncIjpRWgFvc.

○   Compose three or four questions about your own life of prayer and
    activity. You can refer to these questions throughout the week as you
    read and pray.

Week 3, Sunday

PREPARATION

What do you find intriguing about St. Catherine of Siena so far? What do you hope to learn from her?

Read the following gospel passage several times, noting words or phrases that stand out for you. Try to summarize in your own words what Jesus is doing. Imagine your reactions to him as if you were one of those traveling and ministering along with him.

Gospel for the Week: Mark 1:35–39

Rising very early before dawn, he left and went off to a deserted place, where he prayed. Simon and those who were with him pursued him and on finding him said, "Everyone is looking for you." He told them, "Let us go on to the nearby villages that I may preach there also. For this purpose have I come." So he went into their syna-gogues, preaching and driving out demons throughout the whole of Galilee.

Inspiration from St. Catherine

The soul, who is lifted by a very great and yearning desire for the honor of God and the salvation of souls, begins by exercising herself, for a certain space of time, in the ordinary virtues, remaining in the cell of self-knowledge, in order to know better the goodness of God towards her. This she does because knowledge must precede love, and only when she has attained love, can she strive to follow and to clothe herself with the truth. But, in no way, does the creature receive such a taste of the truth, or so brilliant a light therefrom, as by means of humble and continuous prayer, founded on knowledge of herself and of God; because prayer, exercising her in the above way, unites with God the soul that follows the footprints of Christ Crucified, and thus, by desire and affection, and union of love, makes her another Himself. Christ would seem to have meant this, when He said: *To him who will love Me and will observe My commandment, will I manifest Myself; and he shall be one thing with Me and I with him.* In several places we find similar words, by which we can see that it is, indeed, through the effect of love, that the soul becomes another Himself. true, indeed, that the soul unites herself with God by the affection of love.[6]

Prayer for the Week

God who loves us, you filled St. Catherine with such a sense of your love that she was able to live out a productive and joyful life. May her example encourage me to trust your love.

Jesus who became human to be with us, you nourished St. Catherine with your presence, in Eucharist but also in private, deep prayer. May I turn to you always for the nourishment my soul needs.

Holy Spirit, you infused St. Catherine with the wisdom to know the truth and the courage to speak it to anyone who would listen. Continue to work in my soul and prepare me for the words and works God desires from me. Amen.

Week 3, Monday

REMEMBERING OUR SALVATION

Morning Prayer

Scripture: Romans 5:6–11

> For while we were still weak, at the right time Christ died for the ungodly. Indeed, rarely will anyone die for a righteous person—though perhaps for a good person someone might actually dare to die. But God proves his love for us in that while we still were sinners Christ died for us. Much more surely then, now that we have been justified by his blood, will we be saved through him from the wrath of God. For if while we were enemies, we were reconciled to God through the death of his Son, much more surely, having been reconciled, will we be saved by his life. But more than that, we even boast in God through our Lord Jesus Christ, through whom we have now received reconciliation.

Catherine was known to burst into prayers of thanksgiving at just about any time or place, while doing just about anything. Through her conversations with God, she had become increasingly convinced of and captivated by the divine love that chose to dwell with humanity and save it from its own ignorance and tendency to rely on self rather than God. Although she had a well-developed sense of the darkness and hopelessness of a life turned away from God, she was equally aware of how powerful and persistent God's love could be.

She also knew the importance of grasping the plan of salvation—how God works with humanity for our good. Desire for God and understanding of God's activity went hand in hand for a person growing in faith. An entire section of her dialogues describes the "Bridge," referring to Christ's presence with us to bring us back to God. The following excerpts contain some allegorical language that recurs throughout the section: "road of the doctrine," "virtue of the stones," "Bridge."

From St. Catherine

[God speaking in *The Dialogue*] My Goodness, seeing that in no other way could you be drawn to Me, I sent Him in order that He should be lifted on high on the wood of the Cross, making of it an anvil on which My Son, born of human generation, should be re-made, in order to free you from death, and to restore you to the life of grace; wherefore He drew everything to Himself by this means, namely, by showing the ineffable love, with which I love you, the heart of man being always attracted by love.[7]

When He, then, had thus ascended on high, and returned to Me the Father, I sent the Master, that is the Holy Spirit, who came to you with My power and the wisdom of My Son, and with His own clemency, which is the essence of the Holy Spirit. He is one thing with Me, the Father, and with My Son. And He built up the road of the doctrine which My Truth had left in the world. Thus, though the bodily presence of My Son left you, His doctrine remained, and the virtue of the stones founded upon this doctrine, which is the way made for you by this Bridge. For first, He practiced this doctrine and made the road by His actions, giving you His doctrine by example rather than by words; for He practiced, first Himself, what He afterwards taught you, then the clemency of the Holy Spirit made you certain of the doctrine.[8]

Ask Some Questions

1. What attracted me to God initially?

    Catherine's text tells us that we are always attracted by love. What part did love play when I first became intentional about my faith?

2. Can I explain, in fairly simple terms, how God has dealt with humanity, to help and save us?

    Does "Bridge" work for me or are there other terms and phrases that vividly represent God's love through Jesus?

3. What is my experience of love that is one-sided, quite unequal, or unreturned?

    Have I ever loved a person who resisted or refused? When have I hesitated to respond to love, whether a person's or God's?

A Practice

Give yourself some time to linger with a blank page and whatever you want to draw with—pencils, pens, paints. Create an image of Jesus making a connection between you and God the Father/Mother. Perhaps it's a bridge, but create the image that resonates most with you at this point in your life.

Closing Prayer

Lord Jesus, thank you for becoming one of us. Your love

brought you into this human, fragile life. You did it to recon-

cile me and everyone else to God, to the divine life, the healed

life, the joyful life. Amen.

Evening Prayer

o   I take a few deep, slow breaths and invite the Holy Spirit to help me
pray.
o   To do with my body what I hope to do with my spirit, I sit up (or stand),
lift my face to the sky, and open my arms. And I pray: Holy Spirit, help
my spirit open ever more to the beckoning of God's love.

Prayer to St. Catherine

St. Catherine, please stay beside me as I learn to respond

more readily and fully to holy invitations. Amen.

Scripture: Hosea 2:5–6, 8, 14

For their mother has played the whore;
    she who conceived them has acted shamefully.
For she said, "I will go after my lovers;
    they give me my bread and my water,
    my wool and my flax, my oil and my drink."
Therefore I will hedge up her way with thorns;
    and I will build a wall against her,
    so that she cannot find her paths.
. . .
She did not know
    that it was I who gave her

> the grain, the wine, and the oil,
> and who lavished upon her silver
> and gold that they used for Baal.
>
> . . .
>
> Therefore, I will now allure her,
> and bring her into the wilderness,
> and speak tenderly to her.

Hosea the prophet was speaking of God's people and their "adultery" with other gods, from which they sought goods and prosperity. God uses strong language to make the point that the people were unfaithful, acting like people who had no god but needed other gods to help them—like a person who, having a spouse and all they need, decides to look elsewhere. God allows "them" to be stripped naked, showing them shame, allows them to suffer privation. We must keep in mind the culture in which these prophecies occurred, when women were property to their husbands and the worst thing they could do was go to other men. The husband's honor was paramount. God uses this sense of dishonor and shame to evoke in the Israelites the seriousness of their turning to other nations, religions, and idols.

Yet we come to a surprising turn in the story: God the husband will take the wayward wife into the wilderness—away from all other distractions and people—and will "allure" her and "speak tenderly" to her. Even in this brusque Old Testament context, the turning point is God's tender love for those who don't deserve it—for those who, for much of the time, aren't even aware that they need it.

Look for Growth

What might happen when I consider God's plan to bring me into full communion with God the Father, Son, and Holy Spirit?

o   I encounter once again the ongoing invitation to come to my loving God.
o   I benefit from a bird's-eye view of myself—a person who too often has not paid much attention to how badly off I would be were it not for Jesus.
o   The immensity of this salvation story will catch my attention and touch my heart, eliciting joy and gratitude.

Prayer from, or Inspired by, St. Catherine

Oh, Mercy, who proceeds from Your Eternal Father, the Divinity who governs with Your power the whole world, by You were we created, in You were we re-created in the Blood of Your Son. Your Mercy preserves us, Your Mercy caused Your Son to do battle for us, hanging by His arms on the wood of the Cross, life and death battling together; then life confounded the death of our sin, and the death of our sin destroyed the bodily life of the Immaculate Lamb. Which was finally conquered? Death! By what means? Mercy![9]

Gospel Sentence: John 3:16–17

For God so loved the world that he gave his only Son, so that everyone who believes in him might not perish but might have eternal life. For God did not send his Son into the world to condemn the world, but that the world might be saved through him.

Week 3, Tuesday

RESPONDING TO THE EUCHARIST

Morning Prayer

Scripture: Luke 22:14–20

When the hour came, he took his place at table with the apostles. He said to them, "I have eagerly desired to eat this Passover with you before I suffer, for, I tell you, I shall not eat it [again] until there is fulfillment in the kingdom of God." Then he took a cup, gave thanks, and said, "Take this and share it among yourselves; for I tell you [that] from this time on I shall not drink of the fruit of the vine until the kingdom of God comes." Then he took the bread, said the blessing, broke it, and gave it to them, saying, "This is my body, which will be given for you; do this in memory of me." And likewise the cup after they had eaten, saying, "This cup is the new covenant in my blood, which will be shed for you."

Catherine's *Dialogue* features an entire section on the Eucharist. She had practiced extreme fasting from an early age and at times had eaten little more than the holy meal of bread and wine. Living in a time of plague, disease, and death, she saw people waste away from lack of nourishment, in bodies too ill to process food. This vision of starvation was always before her—as it was for most people in those dark times.

Although Catholics today are quick to say that Christ is actually present in the bread and wine, I suspect that believers of Catherine's time felt more desperation for that literal and spiritual nourishment. Keep in mind that not everyone had easy access to the Eucharist. Perhaps we have a better sense of this in the year 2020, as I write this, with the whole world locked down under a deadly pandemic. How many of us long to be physically in church again, able to partake of Christ's Body and Blood? May this deprivation bring us closer to Catherine's sense of the absolute necessity of the Eucharist.

From St. Catherine

See, dearest daughter, in what an excellent state is the soul who receives, as she should, this Bread of Life, this Food of the Angels. By receiving this Sacrament she dwells in Me and I in her, as the fish in the sea, and the sea in the fish—thus do I dwell in the soul, and the soul in Me—the Sea Pacific. In that soul grace dwells, for, since she has received this Bread of Life in a state of grace, My grace remains in her, after the accidents of bread have been consumed. I leave you the imprint of grace, as does a seal, which, when lifted from the hot wax upon which it has been impressed, leaves behind its imprint, so the virtue of this Sacrament remains in the soul, that is to say, the heat of My Divine charity, and the clemency of the Holy Spirit. There also remains to you the wisdom of My only-begotten Son, by which the eye of your intellect has been illuminated to see and to know the doctrine of My Truth, and, together with this wisdom, you participate in My strength and power, which strengthen the soul against her sensual self-love, against the Devil, and against the world. You see then that the imprint remains, when the seal has been taken away, that is, when the material accidents of the bread, having been consumed, this True Sun has returned to Its Center, not that it was ever really separated from It, but constantly united to Me. The Abyss of My loving desire for your salvation has given you, through My dispensation and Divine Providence, coming to the help of your needs, the sweet Truth as Food in this life, where you are pilgrims and travelers, so that you may have refreshment, and not forget the benefit of the Blood. See then how straitly you are constrained and obliged to render Me love, because I love you so much, and, being the Supreme and Eternal Goodness, deserve your love.[10]

Ask Some Questions

1. How do I prepare to receive the Eucharist?
   What do I pray?
   What do I do with my body and my mind before I receive Christ's Body and Blood?

2. When has Communion been especially meaningful or helpful to me?
   What did I experience and how did I respond?

3. What distracts me or makes me hesitate during the Eucharistic liturgy? How might I counteract those impulses?

A Practice

If you are able to partake of the Eucharist soon, take twenty minutes beforehand to meditate on one of the scriptures for today or on the excerpt from *The Dialogue*.

If you are unable to partake of the Eucharist, eat a normal, simple meal on your own and invite Jesus to sit with you. Have a conversation about what it means that his life is in you every day, giving you life and perfecting you.

Closing Prayer

Lord Jesus, renew in my heart thanksgiving and awe at your incarnation, your years of living as one of us and among us— and your continued life within me, every day, through the Holy Spirit's indwelling and through your blessed Body and Blood. Make me hungrier for your presence. Amen.

Evening Prayer

- o I take a few deep, slow breaths and invite the Holy Spirit to help me pray.
- o To do with my body what I hope to do with my spirit, I sit up (or stand), lift my face to the sky, and open my arms. And I pray: Almighty God, continue to refine and perfect me, making me a holy home for your Son. Amen.

Prayer to St. Catherine

St. Catherine, you carried such a vivid sense of Christ-in-you, yet you remained humble and seeking. Accompany me as I cast off distractions and seek Jesus more genuinely. Amen.

Scripture: Isaiah 55:1–3

Ho, everyone who thirsts,
　　come to the waters;
and you that have no money,
　　come, buy and eat!
Come, buy wine and milk
　　without money and without price.
Why do you spend your money for that which is not bread,
　　and your labor for that which does not satisfy?
Listen carefully to me, and eat what is good,
　　and delight yourselves in rich food.
Incline your ear, and come to me;
　　listen, so that you may live.
I will make with you an everlasting covenant,
　　my steadfast, sure love for David.

Look for Growth

What might happen if I celebrate, every day, that Christ's presence sustains and nourishes me?

o   I would experience the Eucharist with more awareness, gratitude, and joy.
o   Lesser "food" would leave me hungering for the real nourishment I need.
o   I would come to see my life with God as a beautiful, ongoing banquet rather than a list of duties to endure.
o   My whole self would grow in perception of God's power in me.

Prayer from, or Inspired by, St. Catherine

Once we have been engrafted into you,

the branches you gave our tree

begin to produce their fruit.

Our memory is filled

with the continual recollection of your blessings.

Our understanding gazes into you

to know perfectly your truth

and your will.

And our will chooses to love and to follow

what our understanding has seen and known.

So each branch offers its fruit to the others.[11]

Gospel Sentence: John 15:4–5

Remain in me, as I remain in you. Just as a branch cannot bear fruit on its own unless it remains on the vine, so neither can you unless you remain in me. I am the vine, you are the branches. Whoever remains in me and I in him will bear much fruit, because without me you can do nothing.

Jesus is our sustenance. We are nourished through the Eucharist, and we are fruitful when we rely on his life in us. But how do we learn to intentionally rely on Christ's life in us? Does it require the stripping away of what does not nourish us?

I confess that my life is sometimes glutted with various foods that don't benefit me—whether too many sweets, too many distracting entertainments, or too many self-indulgent anxieties. I'm full of stuff, which dulls my hunger for what is real and lasting. From time to time, it's good to ask, How hungry am I, really, for the feast God has provided?

Week 3, Wednesday

LOVING OTHERS

Morning Prayer

Scripture: Leviticus 19:18

> You shall not take vengeance or bear a grudge against any of your
> people, but you shall love your neighbor as yourself: I am the LORD.

The verse before Leviticus 19:18 instructs people not to "hate in your heart
anyone of your kin," the idea being that allowing a grievance to simmer
within would probably lead to vengeful action. Where hatred and resentment live, it's difficult for love to grow. We must choose where we spend
our limited energy—in harboring ill feeling or in acting out of love? The
fact that this was included in a section of commandments indicates that we
do have a choice in the matter. We can choose to nurture hatred or love.

From St. Catherine

> All sins are accomplished by means of your neighbor through the
> principles which I exposed to you, that is, because men are deprived
> of the affection of love, which gives light to every virtue. In the same
> way self-love, which destroys charity and affection towards the neigh-
> bor, is the principle and foundation of every evil. All scandals, hatred,
> cruelty, and every sort of trouble proceed from this perverse root of
> self-love, which has poisoned the entire world, and weakened the
> mystical body of the Holy Church, and the universal body of the
> believers in the Christian religion; and, therefore, I said to you, that
> it was in the neighbor, that is to say in the love of him, that all virtues
> were found; and, truly indeed did I say to you, that charity gives life
> to all the virtues, because no virtue can be obtained without charity,
> which is the pure love of Me.[12]

An interesting angle on love of neighbor is lack of judgment. In describing people who live in the perfect light of God's love:

> They find joy in everything. They do not sit in judgment on my servants or anyone else, but rejoice in every situation and every way of living they see, saying, "Thanks to you, eternal Father, that in your house there are so many dwelling places!" And they are happier to see many different ways than if they were to see everyone walking the same way, because this way they see the greatness of my goodness more fully revealed. . . . [E]ven when they see something that is clearly sinful they do not pass judgment, but rather feel a holy and genuine compassion, praying for the sinner and saying with perfect humility, "Today it is your turn; tomorrow it will be mine unless divine grace holds me up."
>
> . . . And because their love is well ordered, dearest daughter, they are never scandalized in those they love, nor in any person, because in this regard they are blind, and therefore they assume no right to be concerned with the intentions of other people but only with discerning my merciful will.
>
> . . . [Y]ou must not pass judgment in your mind, but be concerned only about my will for that person. And if you do see it you must respond not with judgment but with holy compassion. In this way you will attain perfect purity, for if you act this way your spirit will not be scandalized either in me or in your neighbors. For you cast contempt on your neighbors when you pay attention to their ill will toward you rather than my will for them. Such contempt and scandal alienates [sic] the soul from me, blocks her perfection, and to some extent deprives her of grace—in proportion to the seriousness of the contempt and hatred she has conceived for her neighbor because of her judgmental thoughts.[13]

This was God's message to a woman intent on overcoming her own sin and who was quite sensitive to evil in the world, including grave sins in the Church, particularly among the clergy. She was known for confronting powerful men—clergy or rulers—about the truth of situations. Some might say that Catherine's guiding principle was truth, so dedicated she was to living by it and shining a light on it for others.

Yet passing judgment on the person was off limits. When sin was afoot, the correct mode of operation was compassion for the sinner. She could speak the truth and hope that others listened, but discerning others' motives or meanings was for the Lord to do.

Ask Some Questions

1. When do I feel truly loved by another person?
    What words, actions, and attitudes in another make me feel accepted, loved, and safe?

2. When am I most likely to judge others?
    How does my judgment reveal itself in my words and actions?
    What effect does my judgment usually accomplish?
    When others appear to judge me, what is my typical reaction?

3. Catherine writes that love is at the root of all other virtues. How have
    I seen this play out among people I know?

    For instance, when has love enabled a person to be more forgiving
    or truthful, patient or prudent?

    What virtues have grown in me because I have concentrated on
    love for God and for other people?

A Practice

Ask the Holy Spirit to guide you as you remember a time when someone
hurt you or hurt someone you love. Allow yourself to recall details—the
events and the feelings that followed.

Talk to Jesus about the wrong that was done, but try to describe what
happened without referring to anyone's intentions or motives. For instance,
just say, "She did not respond to my letter, even though I needed to hear
from her," rather than, "She had other things to do—I just wasn't important to her." Do you see the difference? State the facts only—because you
have no way of knowing what was really going on in that other person.
Ask Jesus to help you reframe the situation in terms of God's will for every
person involved.

Now, try to pray for that person out of compassion. Ask the Holy
Spirit to help you "be" with the offending person, trying to imagine what
may have been going on for him. "I don't know why he did not respond. I
do know that, during that time, he was having some major problems with
his daughter. And, honestly, he does not have a history of acting hurtfully
toward me. Lord, only you know how he may have been suffering himself."

Closing Prayer

Lord Jesus, you remind us that it's not enough to "do good" to others if we don't regard them as the beloved sons and daughters of God. Help me recognize when I am being judgmental rather than compassionate with people. Amen.

Evening Prayer

o   I take a few deep, slow breaths and invite the Holy Spirit to help me pray.
o   To do with my body what I hope to do with my spirit, I sit up (or stand), lift my face to the sky, and open my arms. And I pray: Lord, show me where love appeared in my life today. Teach me to recognize love so that I may imitate it and learn it. Amen.

Prayer to St. Catherine

St. Catherine, you were so wise, so aware of how evil worked its way into people's lives. But people felt loved in your presence, and you became known as a peacemaker. Help me learn how truth and love go together. Amen.

Scripture: Romans 14:1-4, 10-20, PHILLIPS

Welcome a man whose faith is weak, but not with the idea of arguing over his scruples. One man believes that he may eat anything, another man, without this strong conviction, is a vegetarian. The meat-eater should not despise the vegetarian, nor should the vegetarian condemn the meat-eater—they should reflect that God has accepted them both. After all, who are you to criticise the servant of somebody else, especially when that somebody else is God? It is to his own master that he gives, or fails to give, satisfactory service.

And don't doubt that satisfaction, for God is well able to transform men into servants who are satisfactory. . . .

Why, then, criticise your brother's actions, why try to make him look small? We shall all be judged one day, not by each other's standards or even our own, but by the standard of Christ. It is written: "As I live, says the Lord, every knee shall bow to me, and every tongue shall confess to God." It is to God alone that we have to answer for our actions.

Let us therefore stop turning critical eyes on one another. If we must be critical, let us be critical of our own conduct and see that we do nothing to make a brother stumble or fall.

I am convinced, and I say this as in the presence of Christ himself, that nothing is intrinsically unholy. But none the less it is unholy to the man who thinks it is. If your habit of unrestricted diet seriously upsets your brother, you are no longer living in love towards him. And surely you wouldn't let food mean ruin to a man for whom Christ died. You mustn't let something that is all right for you look like an evil practice to somebody else. After all, the kingdom of Heaven is not a matter of whether you get what you like to eat and drink, but of righteousness and peace and joy in the Holy Spirit. If you put these things first in serving Christ you will please God and are not likely to offend men.

I used J. B. Phillips's paraphrase of these passages because he relates the principle in a more general way; the situation of which Paul was writing had to do with dietary and holy-day differences among Jews and Gentiles, Christians and Jews—and the specifics of the situation are not as important as the concept. Christlike love translates into gentleness; it does not degenerate into argumentation that serves only to hurt others.

Look for Growth

What might happen when I make loving others my first goal of every day?

o   I will notice others in more detail and with more interest rather than allowing them to become part of the landscape.

o I will be intentional about compassion so that it is more than just a nice feeling toward someone—feeling sorry for them—but becomes a way of seeing them as loved by God and therefore worthy of respect.
o I will develop a negative response to my own judgmental thoughts.
o People will notice my attitude and feel safer around me.

Prayer from, or Inspired by, St. Catherine

Lord, how gracious you are with all your beloved people!

In each you see the life of your Son rooted.

You see the Holy Spirit teaching, soothing, and correcting.

Gospel Sentence: Matthew 7:1-3

Stop judging, that you may not be judged. For as you judge, so will you be judged, and the measure with which you measure will be measured out to you. Why do you notice the splinter in your brother's eye, but do not perceive the wooden beam in your own eye?

Much discernment is required when we try to love well. In loving another, I take some responsibility for them. If the love is mutual and there is trust between us, it may fall to me to point out a painful truth to this person I love. After all, love does not stand by and watch a loved one hurt themselves and others. Love speaks up—but in what way?

How do I tell the truth but compassionately?

I make lots of space to listen to that person, which is the only way I can be compassionate, understanding something of what life feels like to them right now and how things look from their perspective. If I am truly loving, that person will feel safe enough with me to be honest about what's going on. If they don't feel safe, then that's on me, not them. I must convey that I accept, respect, and care for them.

In my early life as a Christian, I experienced various relationships that were threatened by forms of spiritual "helping" that were not always helpful. Eventually I came up with a rule for myself: If I felt the need to confront someone about a wrong done to me or an unhealthy pattern I noticed, I would not say anything unless it really hurt me to do so. In other words, if "speaking the truth" to another had the effect of making me feel satisfied, as if I'd gotten something important off my chest, then I had not spoken in love. I had merely participated in spiritualized venting. When I applied this rule, it happened that there were very few situations in which I needed to speak up. When it pained me to say something, but I needed to say it for the good of the other person, then my approach was ever so gentle and certainly not judgmental.

Loving our neighbor involves a lot more than refraining from judgment, but this is an area that is talked about so rarely that it's worth our time of prayer and consideration.

Week 3, Thursday

EMBRACING THE TRUTH

Morning Prayer

Scripture: Jeremiah 6:10–11, 13–14, 16–17

To whom shall I speak and give warning,
    that they may hear?
See, their ears are closed,
    they cannot listen.
The word of the LORD is to them an object of scorn;
    they take no pleasure in it.
But I am full of the wrath of the LORD;
    I am weary of holding it in.

. . .

For from the least to the greatest of them,
    everyone is greedy for unjust gain;
and from prophet to priest,
    everyone deals falsely.
They have treated the wound of my people carelessly,
    saying, "Peace, peace,"
    when there is no peace.

. . .

Thus says the LORD:
Stand at the crossroads, and look,
    and ask for the ancient paths,
where the good way lies; and walk in it,
    and find rest for your souls.
But they said, "We will not walk in it."
Also I raised up sentinels for you:
    "Give heed to the sound of the trumpet!"
But they said, "We will not give heed."

In the prophetic traditions of Judaism and Christianity, the speakers stressed three things: (1) what the situation was—not good, (2) why the situation had fallen to such a state, and (3) what the people must do to rectify the situation. These are three different strands of the truth, or the Truth, as Catherine put it. She understood that when people followed the Truth, things went better. Without being anchored in ultimate reality—that is, God's great mercy, people's tendency to wander from God, and God's continuous invitation for their return and healing—people could float in all sorts of directions, many of them dangerous and harmful.

This was true for ordinary folks getting through the day and for kings and popes making their decisions that would ripple outward.

From St. Catherine

> You know, as I have told you, that, without the light, no one can walk in the truth, that is, without the light of reason, which light of reason you draw from Me the True Light, by means of the eye of your intellect and the light of faith which I have given you in holy baptism, though you may have lost it by your own defects. For, in baptism, and through the mediation of the Blood of My only-begotten Son, you have received the form of faith; which faith you exercise in virtue by the light of reason, which gives you life and causes you to walk in the path of truth, and, by its means, to arrive at Me, the True Light, for, without it, you would plunge into darkness.[14]

Ask Some Questions

1. How am I usually convinced that something is true?

    What are the outward signs, and how does my soul tell me inwardly?

2. When have I witnessed someone (perhaps myself) saying, "Peace, peace" when there is no peace?

    That is, when have I witnessed someone denying a hard truth or when have I lived in denial, and why did I take that route?

3. How have I experienced God's light, which leads to truth?

A Practice

Talk with a mentor or another person of faith who has encouraged you and set an example in the Christian journey. Ask about their experiences of understanding the truth. Talk about denial and other forms of resistance to what God tries to say to us. Pray together about becoming more willing to look at God's light and follow God's truth.

Closing Prayer

Loving God, all of reality is defined by you. If a thing is not from you, then it is false, an illusion. Please help me look directly into your light and love. Help me, Holy Spirit, listen to the truth and go where it leads. Amen.

Evening Prayer

○ I take a few deep, slow breaths and invite the Holy Spirit to help me pray.

○ To do with my body what I hope to do with my spirit, I sit up (or stand), lift my face to the sky, and open my arms. And I pray: Almighty God, guide me in the truth of your love with which you embrace me.

Prayer to St. Catherine

St. Catherine, your experiences of God drew you to follow God's path more closely and attend to God's ways more carefully. You learned to trust the truth rather than be afraid of it. Accompany me as I develop my own trust in God's truth. Amen.

Scripture: James 1:22–25

But be doers of the word, and not merely hearers who deceive themselves. For if any are hearers of the word and not doers, they are like those who look at themselves in a mirror; for they look at themselves and, on going away, immediately forget what they were like. But those who look into the perfect law, the law of liberty, and persevere, being not hearers who forget but doers who act—they will be blessed in their doing.

As we see in the James passage, walking in truth includes consistency between belief and words, words and actions. Integrity is a fundamental aspect of truth. Do I live what I say I believe? Do I convey myself consistently, no matter who I'm with?

Look for Growth

What might happen when I commit myself to the truth—to God's love and light?

o   In deciding to follow truth, I will recognize it more easily, as God gives me the ability to see.
o   I will become more sensitive to falsehood, in myself and in others.
o   I will be less easily tempted to rely on a false self—the person I think I should be rather than the person I am, whom God already loves.
o   I will come to love the light more and more.

Prayer from, or Inspired by, St. Catherine

Your truth said,

"Seek and you shall find;

ask and it shall be given to you;

knock and the door shall be opened to you."

I am knocking at the door of your truth;

I am seeking,

crying out

in the presence of your majesty;

I am pleading to the ears of your clemency

for mercy for the whole world

and especially for holy church.[15]

Gospel Sentence: John 9:41

Jesus said to them, "If you were blind, you would have no sin; but now you are saying, 'We see,' so your sin remains."

We are accustomed to thinking of truth in terms of what is factual and accurate—"the truth." As Christians, we can easily limit our concept of the truth to religious statements. What do the scriptures say about this matter? What is the Church teaching on it? What does the pope say about it? Although this aspect of the truth is important, such proclamations take us only so far. God wants me to receive the light in regard to my own attitudes, words, and actions. Jesus threw harsh light on some people's insistence that they knew the truth while their lives told another story.

Perhaps we should think of the truth not as facts but as light. Light helps us see clearly. For instance, the light of truth shows me that although I am expressing anger, the true emotion from which I'm lashing out is fear. Light reveals what we have kept in the darkness. For instance, my lack of generosity toward someone is rooted envy. Light exposes us but does so for our good. When I know the truth of myself, I can take that truth to prayer rather than present to God the story I've been using to avoid the truth. There's really no grace for a false need. Truth shows us the real need, and God waits to meet us there.

St. Catherine saw the grim truth all around her, in the sick and the destitute, in the people she taught and encouraged, and in the clergy whose lack of truth and integrity threatened the life of the Church in her time. But make no mistake: the truth she first heeded was the light God cast upon her own life. After being schooled herself in truth and light, she was passionate to bring others along that beautiful path with her.

Week 3, Friday

MOVING FROM FEAR TO LOVE

Morning Prayer

Scripture: 1 John 4:18

There is no fear in love, but perfect love casts out fear; for fear has to do with punishment, and whoever fears has not reached perfection in love.

The section of *The Dialogue* about tears is God's answer to Catherine's question about tears, but it's really about phases of a person's spiritual development. To paraphrase: People who live in evil weep because of their state—their evil brings on its own suffering. In a next stage, people recognize their sin and now weep because they fear punishment. When people begin to serve God, their tears are more a response to God's mercy, but they are still in reference to themselves. As they gain in perfection, they love their neighbors and shed tears for the sake of others. As they reach union with God, their tears issue from their joy in God's presence. They do not weep for themselves because they are not the center of their own attention.

From St. Catherine

The soul, exercising herself in virtue, begins to lose her fear, knowing that fear alone is not sufficient to give her eternal life, as I have already told you when speaking of the second stage of the soul. And so she proceeds, with love, to know herself and My goodness in her, and begins to take hope in My mercy in which her heart feels joy. Sorrow for her grief, mingled with the joy of her hope in My mercy, causes her eye to weep, which tears issue from the very fountain of her heart. . . .

[H]er eye, wishing to satisfy the heart, cries with hearty love for Me and for her neighbor, grieving solely for My offense and her neighbor's loss, and not for any penalty or loss due to herself; for she does not think of herself, but only of rendering glory and praise to My Name, and, in an ecstasy of desire, she joyfully takes the food prepared for her on the table of the Holy Cross, thus conforming herself to the humble, patient, and immaculate Lamb, My only-begotten Son.[16]

Here we see the progression from fear to a quality of love that is free of self-concern. But in a critically helpful aside, the Lord says, "And I wish you to know that all these various graces may exist in one soul, who, rising from fear and imperfect love, reaches perfect love in the unitive state." In other words, no one is clearly in one stage or another; rather, we are all making our way through this complex and many-leveled dynamic of letting go of ourselves and receiving God's presence. I suspect that you and I might visit two or three of these stages all on the same day!

Ask Some Questions

1. When was the last time I had a good cry, and what caused those tears?
    Am I aware of tears that are simple responses to pain or frustration as opposed to tears that indicate some positive spiritual movement?
    How do I assess my emotional state with regard to what is happening spiritually?

2. How much fear still resides in my relationship with God?
    How do I recognize when fear is present, and what do I do when that happens?

3. Notice that perfection in a unitive state does not require self-loathing or necessarily self-denial but rather the ability to stop focusing on the self. When have you been able to let go of your self-concern, and what helped you do that?

What might you do to practice letting go of self-concern?

A Practice

Try to finish these sentences as honestly as you can.
"I know you love me, Lord, but . . ."

"I would stop worrying about my own issues if . . ."

"The people on my heart and for whom I pray today are . . ."

Closing Prayer

Holy God, you have made a way for me to walk in perfect love, trusting your grace and letting go of my anxieties. Forgive the gaps in my faith and my lapses into self-interest. Lead me to balance. Amen.

Evening Prayer

○   I take a few deep, slow breaths and invite the Holy Spirit to help me pray.

○   To do with my body what I hope to do with my spirit, I sit up (or stand), lift my face to the sky, and open my arms. And I pray: May I open my hands, my mind, my will, my heart, my future, my emotions, my desires—all to your loving care. Amen.

Prayer to St. Catherine

Dear Catherine, you believed in God's love, which compelled you to treat others with such love and care. I know that love was not always perfect in you, but you kept going, trusting all to God's grace. Your example reminds me that love and fear do not really go together. Thank you. Amen.

Scripture: Romans 8:1–4

There is therefore now no condemnation for those who are in Christ Jesus. For the law of the Spirit of life in Christ Jesus has set you free from the law of sin and of death. For God has done what the law, weakened by the flesh, could not do: by sending his own Son in the likeness of sinful flesh, and to deal with sin, he condemned sin in the flesh, so that the just requirement of the law might be fulfilled in us, who walk not according to the flesh but according to the Spirit.

Look for Growth

What might happen when I learn to identify fear and reject it, focusing instead on God's great love for me?

○   I will begin to recognize when I am operating out of fear and can therefore act against that tendency, with meditation on key scriptures, with prayer, and through talks with a spiritual friend or advisor.

o   The Holy Spirit will meet me in my effort to cast off fear and will remind me of the many graces in my life.
o   My attitude toward others will become less vindictive and more merciful—I won't be focused on people "getting what they deserve" but on their encountering God's love.
o   So many secondary and tertiary anxieties will melt away because they have been fed by my deeper fear of God's judgment.

Prayer from, or Inspired by, St. Catherine

Thanks, thanks be to you, high eternal Godhead,

that you have shown us such great love

by fashioning us with these gracious powers in our soul:

understanding to know you;

memory to keep you in mind,

to hold you within ourselves;

will and love to love you more than anything else.[17]

Gospel Sentence: Luke 11:11–13

What father among you would hand his son a snake when he asks for a fish? Or hand him a scorpion when he asks for an egg? If you then, who are wicked, know how to give good gifts to your children, how much more will the Father in heaven give the holy Spirit to those who ask him?

We know there is such a thing as healthy fear; sometimes, fear of consequences can keep us in line more than our holy sensibility will. But spiritual maturity demands that we develop more and more a holy mindset that is shaped and energized by our relationship with God who loves us. As we become more like Christ, we see the world as he sees it; we are sorrowful for what causes God sorrow; we desire what God desires. At that point, fear dissolves. We are totally convinced that we are in the family now, and God's loving care holds and keeps us. Not only that, we share in God's marvelous work in this world. God moves through our lives, and our lives move by virtue of God's energy in us—transforming love.

Jesus was so convinced of God the Father's love for him that he could continue doing God's will through every kind of hardship. Was Jesus afraid he would be punished if he varied from the plan? We see in Jesus not fear but a steadfast trust in his Father's love and a desire to be united to the Father in whatever work they were doing to heal and redeem the human experience.

God wants that kind of relationship with us. Catherine's description of a unitive state was a way of showing us what it could be like to be that free from fear, free to thrive as beloved sons and daughters. Every facet of this relationship is powered by love.

Catherine's Fire

St. Catherine urged people to see the truth of their lives and God's abundant love. She knew that a person could not bear the truth unless they felt secure in God's love and purpose. If I am confident in God's mercy toward me, then I can deal with the truth of my faults, sins, weaknesses, mistakes, and misperceptions. God's love creates a safe place in which to look honestly at myself and at the world. Catherine's understanding of God's limitless mercy has stoked the courage of people across the centuries: courage to tell the truth, to change their ways, to do the right thing.

Consider your own dealings with truth and faith. How has your concept of reality changed over the years as you've come to love God more and follow Jesus more closely? In what ways have you become more sensitive to truth and falsehood, to integrity and hypocrisy? And how has your growing understanding of the truth influenced your relationship with others?

ST. HILDEGARD OF BINGEN, WHO MODELS ENGAGING LIFE WITH GREAT PASSION AND CREATIVITY

Humans, God made you
in a profoundly sacred space
when the holy Divinity split
Heaven open for the Trinity
to penetrate
and sparkle in earth's muck.
If you want to know why,
look at His humility and kindness.
even the angels who serve God see him in
us who merely walk on
land.[1]

The story of humanity begins with God's desire. It wasn't enough to create the human person; God chose to join divinity with humanity: Incarnation. Through the divine life in us, we are energized to search, learn, understand, imagine, and create. If we could grasp even briefly the majesty of our creation, how much more bravely and kindly might we live? We get an idea of this from St. Hildegard of Bingen.

Week 4, Saturday

WHO WAS HILDEGARD OF BINGEN?

In the year 1099, when Hildegard of Bingen was about one year old, soldiers of the First Crusade took back Christian control of Jerusalem. A few months before her death in September of 1179, a ban against her convent was lifted and the nuns were once again allowed to partake of Mass. The ban was the clergy's response to Hildegard's accepting as pardoned a man whom the Church had excommunicated. Not only her birth and death but just about everything in between developed in the context of social upheaval, religious controversy, and Hildegard's interior conflicts that accompanied significant gifts but also substantial doubts. Yet Hildegard became one of the most accomplished people of her century— not merely the most accomplished *woman* or *Benedictine* but accomplished as compared to anyone of the time.

> Like Saint Francis of Assisi, she composed a harmonious hymn in which she celebrated and praised the Lord *of* and *in* creation. Hildegard united scientific knowledge and spirituality. For a thousand years, she has masterfully taught men and women through her writings, her commentaries and her art. She broke with the customs of her time, which prevented women from study and access to libraries, and, as abbess, she also demanded this for her sisters. She learned to sing and compose music, which for her was a means of drawing nearer to God. For Hildegard, music was not only an art or science; it was also a liturgy.[2]

History is made by each person's responses to their situation, trials, opportunities, and choices. It's safe to say that we cocreate our lives as we respond to God through each moment and circumstance, as we learn to attend to what God is doing within us. In this way, a person born poor and obscure can become a leader of great positive influence; and a person born wealthy with numberless advantages can end up broken and a source of great destruction. Where we begin does not really determine where we go or who we become.

Hildegard's beginning did not necessarily point to the life she cocreated with God. She was the tenth child of a German noble family, and by the time Hildegard was eight years old, her parents determined that she would go the route of the religious life; she was their "tithe" to God. Although the child had no say in the matter, she had already manifested a soul open to God. She had also already experienced visions, which, for the most part, she was afraid to talk about. When she entered the Benedictine community at age fourteen, under the tutelage of Jutta, the anchoress, she was already on a trajectory of holy awareness. Her soul's openness—and, we might also say, fearlessness—prepared this girl's life for astounding productivity and creativity.

We must keep in mind that even for women of noble birth, the options at that time were extremely limited. It was not unusual for a high-born young woman to choose the religious life, which would provide protection and stability, a fair level of education, and a purpose beyond childbearing. Hildegard was conscious throughout her life that her gender kept her from higher levels of education and denied her activities that men enjoyed, such as roles in government and Church leadership. However, she considered these detriments to be proof that her life's wisdom and work must indeed issue from God. In other words, she used her "lowly" position to highlight the veracity of God's activity in and through her.

The list of her accomplishments is astounding: She wrote three major theological works; composed songs and poetry; founded two Benedictine convents; did four preaching tours; and wrote books on plant and animal life, including recipes and instructions on using medicinal herbs. She wrote roughly four hundred letters, to everyone from nuns, priests, and laypeople—including women struggling to get pregnant—to mentors and friends such as St. Bernard of Clairvaux, kings and other public officials, and the pope. One biographer refers to her as a political consultant.

She did all this while chronically ill. We can't know for certain the nature of her illness, but some scholars suspect that she suffered severe migraines. Even so, she lived to the age of eighty-one, which could be considered a minor miracle for that period. Much of her preaching and writing happened during her middle and later years; she seemed to become busier the older she got.

What was Hildegard's appeal? How did a Benedictine untrained as a scholastic capture the attention of monastics across a wide spectrum and gain the approval of a pope before her first theological volume was even completed? Her mystical vision had a lot to do with this. There's a ring of truth to a perception of the universe that integrates the Divine throughout all creation and embraces humanity as a crucial part of the whole.

Hildegard could not deny the truth of her many visions, which had begun during childhood. They instilled in her the sense of what she called "green" energy by which God fills the universe with light and powers God's action through nature, humans, and all creation. Her mystical experience enabled her to step back and see a larger picture of humanity in the context of God's love, light, and power.

She could also speak in a personal, more private voice, often through her songs.

> Shepherd of our souls, and First Voice
> of creation, now let there be . . .
> freedom.
> For we're still wretched creatures,
> always weary, always weak,
> and only You can rescue
> us from the unhappiness
> we make.[3]

Hildegard's visions fueled much of her creative work. However, we cannot underestimate the influence of her ongoing Benedictine life of prayer, work, and relationship with the women for whom she was abbess and the many people with whom she corresponded. Most of us will never have mystical visions, but our lives are fed daily through our own prayer, work, and relationships. Thus this saint can inspire us to dwell deeply in our own experiences of faith and allow God's energy to bring about creative work in whatever form. Hildegard was a poet, musician, theologian, healer, naturalist, and so on. As a Benedictine, she would have been trained in music and literature, and the convent would have become proficient, out of necessity, at using herbal knowledge in the routine treatment of illness. So, her life prepared her for her creative work. Your life and my life prepare us in specific ways to become sources of God's life and creativity. We discover what and how through experience, circumstance, and prayer.

Her message appears extraordinarily timely in today's world, which is especially sensitive to the values that she proposed and lived. For example, we think of Hildegard's charismatic and speculative capacity, which offers a lively incentive to theological research; her reflection on the mystery of Christ, considered in its beauty; the dialogue of the Church and theology with culture, science and contemporary art; the ideal of the consecrated life as a possibility for human fulfilment; her appreciation of the liturgy as a celebration of life; her understanding of the reform of the Church, not as an empty change of structure but as conversion of heart; her sensitivity to nature, whose laws are to be safeguarded and not violated.

For these reasons the attribution of the title of Doctor of the Universal Church to Hildegard of Bingen has great significance for today's world and an extraordinary importance for women. Hildegard expressed the most noble values of womanhood: hence the presence of women in the Church and in society is also illumined by her presence, both from the perspective of scientific research and that of pastoral activity. Her ability to speak to those who were far from the faith and from the Church make Hildegard a credible witness of the new evangelization.[4]

In the week ahead, we will spend time with Hildegard's various sources of holy creativity, meditating on God's communication to us through her, reflecting on our own experience in light of what she has described about God and faith, and focusing our prayer on specific questions to help us follow God's call to our gifts.

Get Ready

Here are some suggestions to prepare for the week:

o   Go online to do some research of your own on Hildegard of Bingen. For instance, "What Can St. Hildegard of Bingen Teach Us? A Look at the Life of This Future Doctor of the Church," October 5, 2012, YouTube video, 2:09, https://www.youtube.com/watch?v=SOveUzIMO10.

o   Compose three or four questions about your own life of faith and creativity. You can refer to these questions throughout the week as you read and pray.

Week 4, Sunday

PREPARATION

What do you find intriguing about St. Hildegard of Bingen so far? What do you hope to learn from her?

Identify what gives you energy and purpose. Is it prayer? Exercise? A hobby? Relationships? Try to list a few sources that help you gain courage to write, sing, teach, or whatever activity has become your gift to the world.

Gospel for the Week: John 6:1–14

After this, Jesus went across the Sea of Galilee [of Tiberias]. A large crowd followed him, because they saw the signs he was performing on the sick. Jesus went up on the mountain, and there he sat down with his disciples. The Jewish feast of Passover was near. When Jesus raised his eyes and saw that a large crowd was coming to him, he said to Philip, "Where can we buy enough food for them to eat?" He said this to test him, because he himself knew what he was going to do. Philip answered him, "Two hundred days' wages worth of food would not be enough for each of them to have a little [bit]." One of his disciples, Andrew, the brother of Simon Peter, said to him, "There is a boy here who has five barley loaves and two fish; but what good are these for so many?" Jesus said, "Have the people recline." Now there was a great deal of grass in that place. So the men reclined, about five thousand in number. Then Jesus took the loaves, gave thanks, and distributed them to those who were reclining, and also as much of the fish as they wanted. When they had had their fill, he said to his disciples, "Gather the fragments left over, so that nothing will be wasted." So they collected them, and filled twelve wicker baskets with fragments from the five barley loaves that had been more than they could eat. When the people saw the sign he had done, they said, "This is truly the Prophet, the one who is to come into the world."

Jesus began with bread and fish and created more. He was not just concerned with the "spiritual" needs of the people but he also tended their earthy needs of body by healing them and feeding them. Hildegard was drawn to the physical reality all around her and perceived that it wove in and out of our spiritual reality. To be "earthy" was to respect and wonder at the spiritual because God had somehow brought all of it together through the very human life of Jesus.

Inspiration from St. Hildegard

O how miraculous is
the foresight of the divine heart,
that foretold every creature.
For when God gazed
upon the face of the human being he had formed
he saw the entirety of all his works
in that same human form.
O how miraculous is the breath
that awakened humankind to life.[5]

Prayer for the Week

God, my Creator, soften my soul, like clay in your hands, to make me pliable to your loving will. Jesus, my Teacher, accompany me as I explore my life for signs of grace, hope, and beauty. Holy Spirit, my Comforter, hover over my life, energizing my spirit to learn and grow. Amen.

Week 4, Monday

FAITH FOUNDATIONS

Morning Prayer

Scripture: Colossians 1:9–14

For this reason, since the day we heard it, we have not ceased praying for you and asking that you may be filled with the knowledge of God's will in all spiritual wisdom and understanding, so that you may lead lives worthy of the Lord, fully pleasing to him, as you bear fruit in every good work and as you grow in the knowledge of God. May you be made strong with all the strength that comes from his glorious power, and may you be prepared to endure everything with patience, while joyfully giving thanks to the Father, who has enabled you to share in the inheritance of the saints in the light. He has rescued us from the power of darkness and transferred us into the kingdom of his beloved Son, in whom we have redemption, the forgiveness of sins.

Because of her originality and creativity, Hildegard has been embraced by some who would play down her orthodoxy. It's safe to say that her words have at times been co-opted by purveyors of non-Christian beliefs, what a few years ago was termed "New Age." However, when we look at the breadth and depth of her work, we find a woman lovingly committed to the foundational tenets of the Christian faith. She interpreted her visions with orthodox belief as the reference point, even when using vocabulary that freshened the view and set her apart from most theologians and teachers of her time. Here is a well-known "description" of the Trinity:

From St. Hildegard

You see "an extremely bright light," which signifies the Father, who is without the stains of illusion, failure, or deceit. And in the light is "the figure of a man the colour of sapphire," which represents the Son, who is without the stains of hard-heartedness, envy or evil, and who before all time, according to his divinity, was begotten of the

Father, but afterwards, in time, according to his humanity, became incarnate in the world. And "it was all burning in a delightful red fire," this is the fire without the stains of aridity, mortality or darkness, which represents the Holy Spirit, by whom the Only Begotten of the Father was conceived in the flesh, born in time of the Virgin and poured out his light, truth and brightness over all the world.

"And the bright light flooded through all the red fire, and the red fire through all the bright light, and the bright light and the red fire shone together through the whole figure of the man so that they were one light in one strength and power." This means that the Father, who is supremely just uniformity, is not without the Son or the Holy Spirit, and that the Holy Spirit, who inflames the hearts of the faithful, is not without the Father or the Son; and that the Son, who is the fullness of fruitfulness, is not without the Father or the Spirit; for they are inseparable in the majesty of divinity, because the Father is not without the Son, nor the Son without the Father, nor the Father or the Son without the Holy spirit, nor the Spirit without them; so these three persons exist as one God in one integral divinity and majesty, and the unity of divinity thrives inseparable in the three persons, because divinity cannot be separated, since it remains always unchanged without any mutability. But the Father is revealed through the Son, the Son through the beginning of created things, and the Holy Spirit through the incarnate Son. How is this? It is the Father who before time engendered the Son; it is the Son through whom all things were created by the Father at the beginning of creation; and it is the Holy Spirit who appeared in the form of a dove at the baptism of the Son of God towards the end of all time.[6]

One of Hildegard's strengths was her ability to perceive the overarching picture of spiritual reality. In book three of her *Scivias*, she provides a lengthy history of humanity's salvation through God's progression of acts, culminating in Jesus.

Vision Ten, section 32: God will bring the Church to her consummation and confound the Devil.

And so, as has been shown, God works from the East to the North to the West to the South, and brings to that consummation which is the last day, for love of the Church in His Son, all that was predestined before the creation of the world. He produces His work through Himself, and draws it back to Himself confirmed and adorned and completed in the highest perfection. . . . When Adam fell, the justice of righteous actions was revived in Noah, surrounded with many miracles, and extended throughout time till the last day. And God did not cease to manifest this by His elect in different times: in the preparation of Noah [east corner], the manifestation in Abraham and Moses [north corner], and the consummation in His Son [west corner]. How? Before time began the desire was in the heart of the Celestial Father to send His Son into the world at the end of time, to save and redeem lost humanity. And the Son, born of the Virgin, fulfilled with a perfect work all things foretold by the Old Testament saints, inspired by the Holy Spirit. . . . And finally it came to perfection in the Son of God, through Whom all the signs and marvels of the old Law were publicly fulfilled, and through Whom all the virtues, which will adorn the heavenly Jerusalem in her children, are declared in the regeneration of the Spirit and water, as the hand with its fingers accomplishes and puts the final touches on a work. . . . For in My Church, which is the mountain of fortitude, I do the work of Justice and sanctity, and destroy you, O shameful impostor. You wanted My people to be destroyed; and you yourself will be conquered and destroyed utterly.[7]

Ask Some Questions

1. When was the last time I thought deeply about the Trinity?

    How does my view of the Trinity influence my prayer life or, for that matter, my spiritual life in general?

2. What place do I give to learning about the Christian story and the Christian faith?

    How well do I understand basic teachings on sin, salvation, redemption, and Christ's work on my behalf?

    More important, how does my understanding of salvation's story make a difference in how I live?

    Or does it?

3. Am I drawn to deeper understanding of spiritual realities?

    If so, how am I drawn, and what might I do to shore up my understanding?

    If I'm not particularly interested in understanding the faith, why is that so?

    Do I think it's impossible to understand so why try?

    What aspects of Christianity do I find difficult to understand or accept?

    Do I avoid thinking about these aspects because they challenge me?

A Practice

Give yourself the gift of a spirituality refresher course. You might read *This Is Our Faith* by Michael Pennock or *The Heart of Catholicism* by Bert Ghezzi. This doesn't have to become a major endeavor. You might go to YouTube for some presentations by a teacher you already know and trust. Some of us have not "learned" about our faith since we were youngsters in Confirmation classes or college students doing coursework. In the intervening years, we have developed the ability to understand our faith with more wisdom and nuance. Revisiting even the basics of the faith can renew and encourage us.

Closing Prayer

Holy Spirit, Jesus sent you to help us, and I know that you dwell in me for that purpose. Guide my thinking and praying as I review what I believe, what the scriptures teach, and what you help me remember and understand. I want my understanding to keep growing and developing. Amen.

Evening Prayer

o   I take a few deep, slow breaths and invite the Holy Spirit to help me pray.
o   To do with my body what I hope to do with my spirit, I sit up (or stand), lift my face to the sky, and open my arms. And I pray: Lord God, this day is coming to an end, and I thank you for bringing me through the hours and to this moment. Quiet my thoughts and open my heart to you. Amen.

Prayer to St. Hildegard

St. Hildegard, your hunger for understanding kept your mind sharp and your spirit open. Please accompany me as I seek to deepen my understanding of how God has dealt with me.

Scripture: 1 Peter 1:10–12

Concerning this salvation, the prophets who prophesied of the grace that was to be yours made careful search and inquiry, inquiring about the person or time that the Spirit of Christ within them indicated when it testified in advance to the sufferings destined for Christ and the subsequent glory. It was revealed to them that they were serving not themselves but you, in regard to the things that have now been announced to you through those who brought you good news by the Holy Spirit sent from heaven—things into which angels long to look!

Look for Growth

What might happen when I explore the mysteries of salvation?

- My memories of encountering God's salvation are refreshed, which can lead to joy.
- I discover a hunger in myself for a deeper connection to God's mysteries.
- The connections between faith and reason are strengthened, helping me feel more integrated.
- My understanding of spiritual matters grows.

Prayer from, or Inspired by, St. Hildegard

O Ruby Blood

O ruby blood

which flowed from on high

where divinity touched.

You are a flower

that the winter

of the serpent's breath

can never injure.[8]

Gospel Sentence: John 3:10–12

Jesus answered and said to him, "You are the teacher of Israel and you do not understand this? Amen, amen, I say to you, we speak of what we know and we testify to what we have seen, but you people do not accept our testimony. If I tell you about earthly things and you do not believe, how will you believe if I tell you about heavenly things?"

Although women religious in the Church's early centuries were not educated nearly to the extent that today's religious are, they were instructed through regular reading of the scriptures, the theology folded within the Divine Offices of prayer, and other "spiritual" reading that was a regular part of daily life. From her youth, Hildegard lived with the anchorite Jutta, whose rooms were attached to the church, and through a window she and young Hildegard could hear the scriptures read, the prayers sung, and any teaching or preaching done in the sanctuary. Hildegard's visions were thus interpreted through the filter of Church teaching.

Anchored in this firm foundation, Hildegard's creativity thrived. She had the freedom to receive amazing visions from God and to allow them to fill in the outlines of doctrine. Her mystical encounters sent her inward in understanding and, at the same time, outward in passion, detail, and description of what she saw and perceived.

Contrary to one popular notion, a belief system does not hinder our spiritual explorations but rather gives us firm footing by which to embark on the journey.

In my years of work with writers and other creatives, I have seen people afraid of their creativity because they thought it might lure them outside the parameters of their faith. In their fear, they forgot that the indwelling Holy Spirit is always willing to guide our work. A good grasp of this theology can free a person to follow where their creative gifts want to take them. For some people, a spiritual practice or ritual sets the stage for the grand exploration of writing, formulating, painting, or sculpting.

Hildegard's various explorations opened for her the faith she was already living. Everything she encountered merely developed in more detail the relationship she had established with God from her earliest years.

Understanding our faith is not a luxury; it is a critical aspect of our formation as people who walk with God. When we understand the basic theology of God-with-us, we are free to discover, day after day, precisely what that means.

Week 4, Tuesday

BODY AND SPIRIT

Morning Prayer

Scripture: Genesis 1:3–4, 27

Then God said, "Let there be light"; and there was light. And God saw that the light was good; and God separated the light from the darkness. . . .

So God created humankind in his image,
in the image of God he created them;
male and female he created them.

Hildegard embraced this human life as a key element in the divine plan. Her description of us stays in line with the Genesis summary of our creation, yet it goes so much further.

From St. Hildegard

And when he created the light, which was winged and could fly everywhere, he determined in the same ancient counsel that he would give a corporeal mass to the spiritual life, which is the breath of life, and give it a shape formed from the clay of the earth, which does not have the ability to fly or breathe or raise itself above itself; therefore it would be all the more bound down and it would gaze all the more attentively towards God. And so the ancient serpent had such hatred for that bond, because this very human creature which had become so weighed down by its corporeality was destined nevertheless, by means of its rationality, to raise itself to the godhead.[9]

In Hildegard's thinking, God made us precisely the way we are for a reason. Her theology of the human person begins with creation, not with our Fall and resultant sinfulness. Furthermore, she does not consider us damaged goods but rather intrinsically related to God by virtue of how we were created. She never plays down the destruction of sin or the hatred of the devil, but none of that really stands up to who we truly are simply because God made us this way.

> Thus God and the human are one, as the soul and the body are one, because human beings are made in the image of God. Everything has its shadow, so too humanity is the shadow of God, and this shadow is the manifestation of all creation. Humanity is thus the manifestation of all God's miracles. The human being is in itself a shadow because it has a beginning. God has neither a beginning nor an end Thus the whole celestial harmony is the mirror of divinity, and humanity is the mirror of all God's miracles.[10]

Ask Some Questions

1. How do I see myself most of the time—as a sinner who needs to be saved or as a person created in the divine image?

    Why do I tend to see myself in one way or the other?

    How can I reconcile the fact of sinfulness with the fact of divinely ordained origins?

2. According to Hildegard, why am I the focus of the "ancient serpent's" hatred? How would I put this in more modern terminology?

3. Am I ever tempted to see the devil as an opposite but equal entity to God?

    Or, to put it another way, do I ascribe to the devil more power than the devil actually has?

    So often, good and evil are described as opposite but also equal, yet it's clear that God's power and purposes are infinite, whereas the devil is but a creature possessing hatred of angelic force. How would I go about each day if I pictured the devil as the ancient serpent rather than a limitless evil force?

A Practice

St. Hildegard taught that "humanity is the mirror of all God's miracles." Using words, paints, movement, or anything that suits you, describe as many miracles as you can that you see in your life.

Closing Prayer

Creator God, please forgive me for taking so lightly my divine origins. They are divine because you created me. Forgive me, too, for seeing myself as a sinner only and not as someone created in your image. I know that I give the sin part too much credit and too much power. You already took care of sin through Jesus, and I know you want me to walk around this world like the image of you that I am. Please help me do that. Amen.

Evening Prayer

○ I take a few deep, slow breaths and invite the Holy Spirit to help me pray.

○ To do with my body what I hope to do with my spirit, I sit up (or stand), lift my face to the sky, and open my arms. And I pray: Help me, Lord, to see myself as wonderfully created and eternally loved. Amen.

Prayer to St. Hildegard

St. Hildegard, thank you for reminding us of who we truly are as beings made in God's image. Amen.

Scripture: Colossians 1:15–20

He is the image of the invisible God, the firstborn of all creation; for in him all things in heaven and on earth were created, things visible and invisible, whether thrones or dominions or rulers or powers—all things have been created through him and for him. He himself is before all things, and in him all things hold together. He is the head of the body, the church; he is the beginning, the firstborn from the dead, so that he might come to have first place in everything. For in him all the fullness of God was pleased to dwell, and through him God was pleased to reconcile to himself all things, whether on earth or in heaven, by making peace through the blood of his cross.

Look for Growth

What might happen if I gaze attentively toward God?

○ I accept that I cannot raise above myself, making way for appropriate humility.

○ I embrace who I am as one whom God created and continues to create every moment.

○ I put myself beyond the power of the devil's hatred.

○ I allow God to gaze back at me, reaching down through my own experience to embrace me.

Prayer from, or Inspired by, St. Hildegard

Creator God,

you honor this human existence by uniting it with your spirit,

"giving a corporeal mass to the spiritual life,

which is the breath of life."

You give your spirit a shape

formed from the clay of the earth.

What glory you give this clay that is my body,

and what brilliance you shine on me

as I live and breathe in these majestic confines

of life on this beautiful earth. Amen.

Gospel Sentence: Mark 5:34

He said to her, "Daughter, your faith has saved you. Go in peace and be cured of your affliction."

It is a tragedy that so many Christians have been conditioned by careless preachers and faulty theology to see their story begin with humanity's Fall. The true beginning of our story is creation, and in the Genesis story, we are the crown of God's creation. Sin and generations of its damage have had their terrible effects, but even that part of the story is eclipsed by Jesus' life, death, and resurrection. As the Colossians passage reminds us, Jesus is the firstborn from the dead, and we follow his lead. Creation is restored, renewed, recreated in grace.

Hildegard's perception of our creation is vivid and dramatic. There's light that has wings, and then there's us! We're the shadow, but we embody all of God's miracles. We're the light without wings that must therefore gaze upward to God because we cannot go there on our own. Our presence is so miraculous that the devil is enraged by it. Surely the devil thought that we were done for, that our taking the bait of sin would condemn us forever, but no. All we need do is look up to the God of all light. In fact,

God made us wingless so we'd have to gaze upward and thus find the One who created us and loves us.

I am weary from watching God's miracles go through life with their eyes downcast. As a spiritual director and retreat leader, I observe how easily we forget who we are. We think we are the most recent sin we committed or that we are the worst thing we've done. In God's expansive design, these matters fall away because *we are who we are created to be*. The irony is that when we focus on our sins, failings, and weaknesses, we are unable to gaze upward. When we cease to look upon our loving Creator, we forget that we remain the lovingly created.

Of course we must deal ruthlessly with the evil that would dog our steps and ruin our days. But must we gaze upon it, remember it, memorialize it, turn it into a spiritual habit? The gaze upward is our means of overcoming what lies at our feet. We must daily, gratefully, joyfully focus on the miracle of our creation and the grace of our re-creation in Christ.

Week 4, Wednesday

JOY IN THE CREATED WORLD

Morning Prayer

Scripture: Psalm 104:14–23

You cause the grass to grow for the cattle,
and plants for people to use,
to bring forth food from the earth,
and wine to gladden the human heart,
oil to make the face shine,
and bread to strengthen the human heart.
The trees of the Lord are watered abundantly,
the cedars of Lebanon that he planted.
In them the birds build their nests;
the stork has its home in the fir trees.
The high mountains are for the wild goats;
the rocks are a refuge for the coneys.
You have made the moon to mark the seasons;
the sun knows its time for setting.
You make darkness, and it is night,
when all the animals of the forest come creeping out.
The young lions roar for their prey,
seeking their food from God.
When the sun rises, they withdraw
and lie down in their dens.
People go out to their work
and to their labour until the evening.

During an era when we are especially aware of humanity's close connection to the rest of creation, it's encouraging to know that wise and holy people have noted this before. The science of ecology and environmentalism is not new, but it's refreshing to find someone such as Hildegard who, in the Middle Ages, took seriously the scientific characteristics of the world. Even today we hear far too much rhetoric that sets science against belief. In Hildegard—along with many others, including writers of the Psalms— we find an easy intertwining of spirit and sense, of the mysterious interior world of love, hope, and belief joined eternally to the mysterious outer world of wind, seeds, muscle and blood, rain and stone.

Hildegard has been celebrated in recent times for her understanding of creation, her closeness to the physical world, and her ability to describe nature in quite spiritual terms.

From St. Hildegard

In its revolving the firmament emits marvellous sounds, which we nevertheless cannot hear because of its great height and expanse; likewise a millwheel or cartwheel gives off sounds when it turns. But the firmament is at such a height and expanse above the earth so that it does not destroy the people and animals upon the earth; therefore it is far enough away, for if it were any nearer the humans and animals would perish by the fire and winds and by the water and the clouds. As body and soul are one and support each other, in the same way the planets with the firmament confirm each other and strengthen each other. And like the soul that enlivens and strengthens the body, the sun with the moon and the other stars—warms and strengthens the firmament with its fire. Thus the firmament is like a human head; the sun, moon and stars are the eyes; the air is our sense of hearing, the winds our sense of smell, the dew our taste; the sides of the cosmos are like our arms and our sense of touch. And the other creatures that are in the world are like our stomach, but the earth is our heart. As the heart holds the body together from top to bottom so the earth is a secure land for the waters on its surface and a firm resistance to the waters beneath the earth to prevent them from wrongly breaking out.[11]

Ask Some Questions

1. In what ways do I connect, on a regular basis, with the natural world?

2. When did I last linger with creation enough to be filled with awe, joy, or curiosity?

3. In what ways is my spiritual life fed by the natural world?
   How can I more intentionally dwell upon the physical universe so that God can impress me with its wisdom and wonder?

A Practice

Choose a documentary or book that expounds on some part of the natural world. Before you begin watching or reading, light a candle and pray something such as this: Heavenly Father, you created me and the world I live in. May I partake of this information as though it were another kind of scripture, yet another way for you to speak to me and reveal yourself to me. I wait in expectation and gratitude. Amen.

Closing Prayer

Lord Jesus, this universe exists through you, just as I exist through you. If your love ceased, everything would fly apart and would be no more. Thank you for holding together this grand universe with your love and power. Amen.

Evening Prayer

○   I take a few deep, slow breaths and invite the Holy Spirit to help me pray.

○   To do with my body what I hope to do with my spirit, I sit up (or stand), lift my face to the sky, and open my arms. And I pray: God, my creator and father/mother, thank you for placing me in this stunning world. Forgive me for the moments I forget to stand in awe of it. Amen.

Prayer to St. Hildegard

St. Hildegard, may my soul taste

the kind of curiosity you experienced

in regard to the numberless wonders all around me. Amen.

Scripture: Romans 8:19–22

For the creation waits with eager longing for the revealing of the children of God; for the creation was subjected to futility, not of its own will but by the will of the one who subjected it, in hope that the creation itself will be set free from its bondage to decay and will obtain the freedom of the glory of the children of God. We know that the whole creation has been groaning in labor pains until now.

Look for Growth

What might happen when I see the whole universe as a means of God revealing God's self?

o   I perceive the universe as a friendly and beautiful place.
o   I am reminded that God is present in every plant and particle—that I am surrounded by and enfolded in God's majestic presence.
o   Nature itself inspires me to kindness toward every creature.
o   Every location, whether a lone flowerbox on a city balcony or a summer meadow in the countryside, becomes a place of worship.

Prayer from, or Inspired by, St. Hildegard

God is the foundation for everything

This God undertakes, God gives.

Such that nothing that is necessary for life is lacking.

Now humankind needs a body that at all times honors and

praises God.

This body is supported in every way through the earth.

Thus the earth glorifies the power of God.[12]

Gospel Sentence: Matthew 6:28–29

Why are you anxious about clothes? Learn from the way the wild flowers grow. They do not work or spin. But I tell you that not even Solomon in all his splendor was clothed like one of them.

I grew up in a tiny Kansas town surrounded by farmland. At age thirty, I was delighted to be transplanted in Chicago, where I attended grad school. I loved the city from my first glimpse of its famous skyline from my seat on the commuter train. The diverse and busy population, the clatter and hum of trains and buses, the architectural genius showcased down the lakefront, along Michigan Avenue, and on either side of the river branches downtown—all of it stimulated my senses and woke me up to each day with great curiosity. There was always something happening! And the view was constantly changing as people moved about and buildings were erected and parades processed through the yearly events and holidays.

During my thirty years in that city, I learned to recognize creation wherever I found it. Vining flowers on our third-story porch, the trees bowing over the hundreds of small city parks that were created for an urban population that included many people who did not have their own backyards but lived in apartments surrounded by concrete and asphalt. I said a prayer of thanks every time I walked along the lakefront in Grant Park, one of the largest public spaces on a waterfront in the whole country. Decades earlier, city planners understood the importance of every citizen having access to a lake view, a park bench, or a shade tree. My entire time in Chicago, I never "owned" property that came close to the large, leafy backyards of my country childhood, but I found creation everywhere—because I looked for it, no longer taking it for granted.

A lot of people who read this book will be urban dwellers. If you are one of those people, please know that creation has a way of breaking through the cracks in sidewalks or peeking in apartment windows twenty stories up. The clouds will find you, as will the rain and sun, the thunder and snow, the fragrance of green things growing even if they are blocks away. You can create a sanctuary with one flowerpot, and a folding chair on that balcony above the concrete can give you a front-seat view of heaven.

Dare to sit with your soul until you perceive its longing for the universe. Notice that something within you hungers after the stars, that a part of you recognizes a secret in the soft eye of a mourning dove on the nearby wall. Allow your hunger for the universe to well up and seek the wonders quite near you. We are meant to have this hunger because it draws us close to the whole of God's creation.

Week 4, Thursday

THE BEAUTY OF SONG

Morning Prayer

Scripture: Psalm 33:1–3

Rejoice in the LORD, O you righteous.
Praise befits the upright.
Praise the LORD with the lyre;
make melody to him with the harp of ten strings.
Sing to him a new song;
play skillfully on the strings, with loud shouts.

As a member of a Benedictine community, Hildegard would have been familiar with liturgical chant. She would have heard such music and sung it regularly. It's not surprising that she would write songs devoted to the Virgin Mary, the angels, and so forth. But as with her other creative work, Hildegard's songs present fresh images and phrases on which to meditate. A simple online search will bring up lists of her chants and songs performed by a variety of artists. I encourage you to listen to a few, whether with singing or only instrumental:

"Lumière Vivante—Chants de Hildegarde de Bingen," July 23, 2016, YouTube video, 2:18, https://www.youtube.com/watch?v=YG6li5LQoRU.

"Hildegard von Bingen," Last.fm, https://www.last.fm/music/Hildegard+von+Bingen.

From St. Hildegard

Holy Spirit, quickening life,
moving all things, the root in all creation,
who washes all things of impurity,
removing sins and soothing wounds
who is shining light and laudable life,
wakening and reawakening all things.

Love abounds in all things,
excels from the depths to beyond the stars,
is lovingly disposed to all things.
She has given the king on high
the kiss of peace.

Angels, living light most glorious!
Beneath the Godhead in burning desire
in the darkness and mystery of creation
you look on the eyes of your God
never taking your fill:
What glorious pleasures take shape within you
and remain intact from all the evil work
which first arose in your companion,
the angel of perdition,
who wished to soar
above the inward hidden pinnacle of God.
From there he fell, and plunged to his destruction;
and yet he delivered
the instruments of his fall
to the work of God's finger.[13]

The song of rejoicing softens the hard heart and summons the Holy Spirit.

For the song of rejoicing softens hard hearts, and draws forth from them the tears of compunction, and invokes the Holy Spirit. And so *those voices you hear are like the voice of a multitude, which lifts its sound on high;* for jubilant praises, offered in simple harmony and charity, lead the faithful to that consonance in which is no discord, and make those who still live on earth sigh with heart and voice for the heavenly reward.

And their song goes through you so that you understand them perfectly; for where divine grace has worked, it banishes all dark obscurity, and makes pure and lucid those things that are obscure to the bodily sense because of the weakness of the flesh.[14]

Ask Some Questions

1. When has music stirred me spiritually?
   What was the situation? How did I respond?

2. Which songs would I place on my list of "spiritual encouragement" songs? These are songs that lift me up when I'm down, that support my faith when it wavers, that remind me of what I already believe.

3. If I could write a song to God, what would it say?

A Practice

Write a song to God. Come up with a few phrases that say what you want to say. They don't have to be wonderful poetry, but they should ring true to what is in your heart. Then put them to music. It can be music you create or—if you are sure you can't come up with your own tune—music that you already know from somewhere else. This is just for your prayer, so you can use whatever you want.

Sing this song until you can do it easily, by memory. Then you can truly engage your heart as you sing it.

Closing Prayer

Holy Spirit, you inspired St. Hildegard in so many ways, and her songs have blessed the world for centuries. Thank you for the beauty and wisdom of her many songs. Thank you for tunes that lift the spirit to God. Amen.

Evening Prayer

o   I take a few deep, slow breaths and invite the Holy Spirit to help me pray.
o   To do with my body what I hope to do with my spirit, I sit up (or stand), lift my face to the sky, and open my arms. And I pray: Help me, Lord, to free myself to sing to you, without worry or self-consciousness. May my voice express the love that is in my heart. Amen.

Prayer to St. Hildegard

St. Hildegard, help me pause for a song and take joy in its words and melody. Amen.

Scripture: Colossians 3:12–17

As God's chosen ones, holy and beloved, clothe yourselves with compassion, kindness, humility, meekness, and patience. Bear with one another and, if anyone has a complaint against another, forgive each other; just as the Lord has forgiven you, so you also must forgive. Above all, clothe yourselves with love, which binds every-thing together in perfect harmony. And let the peace of Christ rule in your hearts, to which indeed you were called in the one body. And be thankful. Let the word of Christ dwell in you richly; teach and admonish one another in all wisdom; and with gratitude in your hearts sing psalms, hymns, and spiritual songs to God. And whatever you do, in word or deed, do everything in the name of the Lord Jesus, giving thanks to God the Father through him.

Look for Growth

What might happen when I use songs and music in my spiritual life?

o   I engage my physical senses as I communicate to God and others.
o   My mind, body, and emotions come to memorize musical expressions of faith.
o   My faith connects deeply with my emotions as well as my thoughts.
o   I can involve others in this holy communication—we can all sing together!

Prayer from, or Inspired by, St. Hildegard

Praise to the Trinity—the sound and life

and creativity of all within their life,

the praise of the angelic host

and wondrous, brilliant splendor hid,

unknown to human minds, it is,

and life within all things.[15]

Gospel Sentence: Matthew 11:16–17

To what shall I compare this generation? It is like children who sit in marketplaces and call to one another, "We played the flute for you, but you did not dance, we sang a dirge but you did not mourn."

St. Hildegard's grasp of faith, the human person, and Christian theology earned her the designation Doctor of the Church. But hers was a holistic experience of the Divine, which combined passion, emotion, poetry, and the physical senses with reason, doctrine, and history. It was not enough to write about the Trinity; she also had to sing about the Trinity. A life overflowing with the experience of God naturally relates this experience in every way possible.

Many of us grow up learning to sing or play an instrument, and often we use our musical skills in worship and retreat settings. There's also a social aspect to our "spiritual songs" because we are accustomed to singing with others—in some cases, rehearsing regularly with a choir.

I would challenge us, though, to explore song in our private devotion—to sing as part of our prayer. Perhaps learn to chant the psalms or other scriptures. We now know that from a medical standpoint, our health benefits from the vibrations that happen in the body when a person sings or chants. Singing is a way to do with the body what we are doing in the spirit—yet another way for us to integrate body and soul.

For some of us, it's easier to sing our prayers than to speak them. I suspect that quite a few people learned to express their hearts to God by writing those expressions into song form. That's certainly when my own prayer began to develop a life of its own. I was probably ten at the time, and for at least a decade my primary prayer happened when I sang my soul at the piano, alone and searching for the right words, developing the courage to sing them.

May your experience of God overflow your heart and spill out with your voice!

Week 4, Friday

DISCERNMENT OF INNER WORKINGS

Morning Prayer

Scripture: Psalm 42:9–11

I say to God, my rock,
  "Why have you forgotten me?
Why must I walk about mournfully
  because the enemy oppresses me?"
As with a deadly wound in my body,
  my adversaries taunt me,
while they say to me continually,
  "Where is your God?"

Why are you cast down, O my soul,
  and why are you disquieted within me?
Hope in God; for I shall again praise him,
  my help and my God.

It does little good to understand God's intentions toward us, to perceive God's mercy, and to respond to God's invitation if we don't also learn to understand ourselves. How do we read what goes on inside mind and heart? How can we learn to notice interior patterns and pitfalls so as to make wiser choices as we go along?

Why not become wise about what makes us tick? About what helps or hinders our spiritual progress? We can respond to God's mercy and receive it, but unless we know ourselves, that wonderful grace will not produce as much fruit as it desires to do. Without attention to our inner workings, we fall into self-deception, even self-sabotage.

At first glance, St. Hildegard's "morality" play about the virtues seems idealistic and melodramatic. Morality plays as they developed during the Middle Ages were highly allegorical and, well, preachy. But a closer read of this play about the virtues reveals insight into a person's interior struggles. We hear a long discussion among the penitent soul, the virtues, humility, and the devil. We feel the wavering back and forth of the penitent, who needs the encouragement of the virtues and the assistance of humility to turn back to God. Below are just a few verses.

From St. Hildegard

The Lament of the Penitent Soul, in the Body, Calling on
    the Virtues:
Royal Virtues!
How beautiful and bright you are in the height of the sun
And how sweet is your habitation.
And how terrible for me that I have fled from you!

Virtues:
Return, fugitive! Return to us,
And God will receive you!

The Penitent Soul in the Body:
Ah, I have been swallowed up by the terrible sweetness of sins!
I have not dared to return!

Virtues:
Do not fear and do not flee,
For you are the lost sheep whom the Good Shepherd is seeking.

The Penitent Soul in the Body:
Now I need you to receive me back,
Because I stink from the wounds
With which the ancient serpent has defiled.

Virtues:
Run to us,
Follow the footsteps in which you will never fall
with us as your companions,
And God will heal you.

The Penitent Soul in the Body:
I am a sinner who fled from Life:
Covered with sores I return to you,
That you may offer me the shield of redemption.

Virtues:
Runaway soul, be strong,
And put on the armour of light.
. . .
Humility to the Virtues:
All you virtues,
Receive this sinner in mourning, with all her scars,
For the sake of the wounds of Christ,
And lead her to me.

Virtues to the Penitent Soul in the Body:
We will take you back
And we will not desert you,
And all the host of heaven will be glad for you:
Now is the time to sound forth in harmony.

Humility to the Penitent Soul:
Unhappy daughter, I will embrace you:
The great healer has suffered hard and bitter wounds
For your sake.

Devil:
Who are you? Where have you come from?
You embraced me,
And I led you out
Now you confound me in your reversal,
But I will throw you down in my struggle!

Penitent Soul Rejecting the Devil:
When I realized all your ways were evil
I fled from you,
But now, deceiver,

I fight against you.

Penitent Soul to Humility:
Therefore, Queen Humility,
Help me with your medicine![16]

Then Humility appeals to the help of the virtues, who fight against and
bind the deceiver. The return of a penitent soul relies on reason, encouragement, assistance, and battle. All of this is interior action, the movements
in a person that take them one way or another.

Even more fascinating is Hildegard's lengthy description of how the
Grace of God works upon humans—from book 3, Vision Eight:

8. Words of the Grace of God, to admonish humans

But many of these people recognize me [the Grace of God]. How?
When I begin to touch them, one of them may say to himself, "What is
happening to me? I know nothing of good and am incapable of thinking of it." And then, in his ignorance, he sighs and says, "Alas for me,
a sinner!" But he feels nothing more, because he is weighed down
by his huge weight of sin, and the darkness of iniquity troubles him.
Then I touch his wounds again. And, having been admonished by
me before, he understands me better this time, and looks at himself,
saying, "Woe is me! What shall I do? I do not know and cannot think
what will become of me for my many sins. Oh, where shall I turn,
and to whom shall I flee, who can help me cover over my shameful
crimes and efface them by repentance?"

And again he looks at himself, with the same turbulence that
formerly propelled him into sin; and then he turns to true repentance,
with a desire as great as his former eagerness to sin. And as this
person, by my warning, thus wakes from the sleep of death, which
he had preferred to life, he no longer desires to sin by thought, word
or deed, which before were ardently directed toward crime. And in
strong repentance he rises to me; and I wholly receive him, and from
henceforward discharge him as free. He will no longer be troubled
by the aforesaid things, which I use to warn my dearest children to
hold out against the fiery arrows of the Devil's persuasion; for he

no longer needs them. For he will always sorrow at the sins he has committed, and in his self-scorn he will do such severe penance that he will deem himself unworthy to be called human. And this victory comes out of the stench of those filthy people, whom I choose not to cast out; for after sinning they have sought me. I am prepared to do anything they ask for those who do not spurn me but receive my admonition and devoutly seek me. But those who despise and reject me are dead, and I do not know them.[17]

Ask Some Questions

1. What are the various voices holding discussions inside me?

    How do I identify a voice that helps and encourages, and when do I realize that the speaker is working against me with accusations and shame?

2. When have I perceived God's grace touching me, causing me to examine what I'm doing or where I'm headed?

    How has grace spoken to me—through a dream or a feeling, through a friend or something I read?

3. Do I recognize when my own soul is hurting or in danger and longing
    to change course?

    If so, how do I recognize the signals?

A Practice

Ask the Holy Spirit to hover over this imaginative experiment you're about
to do.

Draw a picture of a round table. Around that table, draw figures that
represent the voices echoing inside you. You might call one Conscience,
another Fear; one Shame, another Faith. One "person" sitting at the table
may be the grandmother who always saw the best in you; another could
be the person who robbed you of joy when you were very young.

Be sure to give Grace a seat at the table—you will need her as this
discussion gets going!

Allow these presences to speak. Hear them out so that you can understand why they are even at this table, in your soul. For instance, why does
Fear keep showing up? Perhaps you can observe and listen while Faith
talks with Fear.

This exercise will take some time, and you may need to return to it a
few times before you can relax and allow the conversation to happen.

Closing Prayer

Loving God, you have given me the ability to speak with my

own soul, to reflect on my thoughts and feelings, and to grow

in understanding of how you work within me. Thank you,

thank you for this. Amen.

Evening Prayer

o   I take a few deep, slow breaths and invite the Holy Spirit to help me pray.
o   To do with my body what I hope to do with my spirit, I sit up (or stand), lift my face to the sky, and open my arms. And I pray: Holy Spirit, teach my soul to hear you and respond to your promptings. Amen.

Prayer to St. Hildegard

St. Hildegard, it seems that you were quite fearless about delving into the soul. I'm not quite so brave, but if you walk with me, I'll try to pay better attention to what's happening in me. Amen.

Scripture: Romans 12:2–3

Do not be conformed to this world, but be transformed by the renewing of your minds, so that you may discern what is the will of God—what is good and acceptable and perfect.

For by the grace given to me I say to everyone among you not to think of yourself more highly than you ought to think, but to think with sober judgement, each according to the measure of faith that God has assigned.

Look for Growth

What might happen when I attend to the conversations and movements in my soul?

o   I learn to distinguish between different voices, identifying words that come from faith as opposed to fear, for instance.
o   My sensitivity to spiritual understanding is heightened.
o   The Holy Spirit has greater opportunity to teach me wisdom because I am paying attention to my true feelings, thoughts, images, and beliefs.
o   Self-awareness will lead to spiritual confidence as I learn to recognize my unique spiritual processes.

Prayer from, or Inspired by, St. Hildegard

Loving God, I fled from your life and light.

Wandering in this state, I gathered so many wounds.

The enemy took advantage, and I felt defenseless.

I need for you to receive me back.

Please gather me in your arms

and heal me. Amen.

Gospel Sentence: John 8:31–32

Jesus then said to those Jews who believed in him, "If you remain in my word, you will truly be my disciples, and you will know the truth, and the truth will set you free."

Trained by the disciplines of life in the Benedictine order and seasoned by her duties as an abbess who must oversee the well-being of her nuns, Hildegard of Bingen became an astute observer of spiritual movement in herself and others. She was considered wise enough to do tours of preaching and advise people from every walk of life. Her writings reveal to us at least some of the detail and diligence she applied to her growing understanding of human nature, the wider universe, and God as revealed through scripture and prayer.

Were these gifts of understanding pressed upon her from those earliest visions in her childhood, compelling her into a life of revelations? Or was she simply brave enough to be curious about topics considered too immense and wonderful for the human mind to approach? Perhaps her strong curiosity joined forces with God's graces at just the right place and time to result in the astounding life she came to live.

Hildegard's Fire

Because St. Hildegard engaged fully and with detailed attention to so many aspects of her life, the world is gifted with her works of vivid insight and beauty, whether theological essays or devotional songs. Her openness to and wonder at God's universe has encouraged generations of God seekers to encounter divine presence and love in a starry sky or the body's breath. Her curiosity continues to refresh and challenge us.

What are you and I to do with the offerings of this long-ago woman but very present saint? I think she would encourage us to open our eyes and ears, our minds and hearts, and expect God to meet us in the unique circumstances of our lives. She would tell us to be humble in our prayers before God, who will lead us into courageous action and creativity.

Do we dare listen to our souls and attend to the drama within—the ever-present motion between self and Creator, between consciousness and Holy Spirit, between our fragile body and the incarnate Christ? Can we simply be here, where we are, fully engaged in this moment's thought and breath? Hildegard described light, fire, music, and movement in this world. She could describe those wonders because she lingered with God long enough and often enough to perceive them, to ponder them, and eventually to write about them for our benefit.

We have our own praying to do. Our own pondering and sensing. The results of our lingering with God will come forth in so many ways—songs and stories, inventions and cures, programs of compassion and structures for social change. Who knows what will happen when we commune with our Creator and learn who we truly are!

TO CLOSE

God worked out a specific life for each of these wise women, these Doctors of the Church with whom we have walked for four weeks. Divine love embraced each in the mystery of her personality, history, temperament, and historical situation. It would be interesting to put them all in a room together, wouldn't it, just to see how these four graced lives might interact and what new wonders would be the result. I suspect that they are keeping one another company now, along with the rest of our great cloud of witnesses who have already left this life and gone to be with God in yet another phase of this existence we've been given.

I encourage you to take some deep breaths as you exit this season of prayer with Thérèse, Teresa, Catherine, and Hildegard. Give yourself time to hold in memory what has transpired. Review your journal, if you kept one. Savor the graces of the past few weeks.

Also, resist the temptation to compare yourself too closely with these or any saints. Their legacy is for your benefit, and there is much to gain from their words. But God is just as interested in your specific life blooming according to who you are in this space and time as God was focused upon each of these women in her time and place.

May this prayer experience set you more firmly on your own path with the Lord Jesus, with the Holy Spirit, with your Father/Mother God. May you be inspired by Thérèse's childlike receptivity, Teresa's spiritual courage, Catherine's fight for truth, and Hildegard's celebration of life. You will find the life focus best suited to you, and even if you don't follow a path anything like these saints, the same divine love will guide and shape you.

These lovely women, along with the God they love, invite you to become who you are meant to be. Then you will set the world on fire as only you can.

You can be certain that these four graced women will be cheering you on.

NOTES

To Begin

1. John Paul II, "Proclamation of St Thérèse of the Child Jesus and the Holy Face as a 'Doctor of the Church,'" Libreria Editrice Vaticana, October 19, 1997, sec. 3, https://www.vatican.va/content/john-paul-ii/en/homilies/1997/documents/hf_jp-ii_hom_19101997.html.

Week 1: St. Thérèse of Lisieux

1. Thérèse of Lisieux, *Story of a Soul (L'Histoire d'une Ame): The Autobiography of St. Thérèse of Lisieux*, ed. T. N. Taylor (London, 1912), 17. Available through Christian Classics Ethereal Library, https://www.ccel.org/ccel/therese/autobio.html.

2. John Paul II, "Proclamation of St Thérèse of the Child Jesus and the Holy Face as a 'Doctor of the Church,'" Libreria Editrice Vaticana, October 19, 1997, paras. 4–5, https://www.vatican.va/content/john-paul-ii/en/homilies/1997/documents/hf_jp-ii_hom_19101997.html.

3. Francis, "Apostolic Journey of His Holiness Pope Francis to Georgia and Azerbaijan," Holy Mass at Mikheil Meskhi Stadium, Tbilisi, October 1, 2016, https://www.vatican.va/content/francesco/en/homilies/2016/documents/papa-francesco_20161001_omelia-georgia.html.

4. Thérèse of Lisieux, "Just as the Sun Shines," Society of the Little Flower, September 12, 2013, https://blog.littleflower.org/tag/st-therese-quotes/page/3/.

5. Thérèse of Lisieux, *The Story of a Soul*, trans. and ed. Robert J. Edmonson (Brewster, MA: Paraclete Press, 2006), 274.

6. Thérèse of Lisieux, *Story of a Soul (L'Histoire d'une Ame)*, 234.

7. Thérèse of Lisieux, *The Story of a Soul*, 230–31.

8. "Prayers of St. Thérèse," Our Catholic Prayers, accessed August 23, 2021, https://www.ourcatholicprayers.com/prayers-of-st-therese.html.

9. Elizabeth A. Dreyer, *Accidental Theologians: Four Women Who Shaped Christianity* (Cincinnati, OH: Franciscan Media, 2014), 97.

10. Thérèse of Lisieux, *The Story of a Soul*, 172–73.

11. Thérèse of Lisieux, *Story of a Soul (L'Histoire d'une Ame)*.

12. Thérèse of Lisieux, *Story of a Soul (L'Histoire d'une Ame)*, 150.

13. Thérèse of Lisieux, *Story of a Soul (L'Histoire d'une Ame)*, 241.

14. Thérèse of Lisieux, *Story of a Soul (L'Histoire d'une Ame)*, 119–20.

Week 2: St. Teresa of Ávila

1. Carmen Acevedo Butcher, *Incandescence: 365 Readings with Women Mystics* (Brewster, MA: Paraclete Press, 2005), 37.

2. Benedict, "Saint Teresa of Avila," Libreria Editrice Vaticana, February 2, 2011, https://www.vatican.va/content/benedict-xvi/en/audiences/2011/documents/hf_ben-xvi_aud_20110202.html.

3. Francis, "Letter of the Holy Father to the Superior General of the Order of Discalced Carmelites on the 500th Anniversary of the Birth of Saint Teresa of Jesus," Libreria Editrice Vaticana, March 28, 2015, https://www.vatican.va/content/francesco/en/letters/2015/documents/papa-francesco_20150328_lettera-500-teresa.html.

4. Elizabeth A. Dreyer, *Accidental Theologians: Four Women Who Shaped Christianity* (Cincinnati, OH: Franciscan Media, 2014), 80.

5. Teresa of Ávila, *The Way of Perfection*, as quoted in Butcher, *Incandescence*, 100.

6. Teresa of Ávila, *The Interior Castle, or The Mansions* (Grand Rapids, MI: Christian Classics Ethereal Library), 20.

7. Teresa of Ávila, *The Way of Perfection*, trans. Henry L. Carrigan, Jr. (Brewster, MA: Paraclete Press, 2009), 149.

8. Teresa of Ávila, *Interior Castle, or the Mansions*, 98.

9. Teresa of Ávila, *Way of Perfection*, 68–69.

10. *Autobiography of St. Teresa of Avila*, trans. E. Allison Peers (Mineola, NY: Dover Publications, 2010), 70.

11. Prayers of St. Teresa of Jesus (Ávila), Boston Carmel, carmelitesofboston.org.

12. *Autobiography of St. Teresa of Avila*, 25.

13. *Autobiography of St. Teresa of Avila*, 70.

14. *Autobiography of St. Teresa of Avila*, 50.

15. *Autobiography of St. Teresa of Avila*, 40–41.

16. Teresa of Ávila, *Interior Castle, or The Mansions*, 34.

17. Teresa of Ávila, *Way of Perfection*, 107.

18. Teresa of Ávila, *Interior Castle, or The Mansions*, 27–28.

Week 3: St. Catherine of Siena

1. Catherine of Siena, *The Dialogue*, trans. and ed. Suzanne Noffke (Mahwah, NJ: Paulist Press, 1980), 29.

2. *Butler's Lives of the Saints.*

3. Catherine of Siena, *Dialogue*, 9.

4. Benedict XVI, "Saint Catherine of Siena," Libreria Editrice Vaticana, November 24, 2010, https://www.vatican.va/content/benedict-xvi/en/audiences/2010/documents/hf_ben-xvi_aud_20101124.html.

5. "Pope Francis: May Catherine of Siena Protect Italy and Europe," Vatican News, April 29, 2020, https://www.vaticannews.va/en/pope/news/2020-04/pope-at-audience-may-catherine-of-siena-protect-italy-and-europ.html.

6. *The Dialog of Catherine of Siena* (London: Kegan Paul, Trench, Trubner, 1907), 17. Available through Christian Classics Ethereal Library, https://www.ccel.org/ccel/catherine/dialog.

7. *Dialog of Catherine of Siena*, 47.

8. *Dialog of Catherine of Siena*, 52.

9. *Dialog of Catherine of Siena*, 55.

10. *Dialog of Catherine of Siena*, 143.

11. *The Prayers of Catherine of Siena*, trans. and ed. Suzanne Noffke (New York: Authors Choice Press, 2001), "Prayer 17," 177.

12. *The Dialogue of St. Catherine of Siena* (New York: Magisterium Press, 2015).

13. Catherine of Siena, *Dialogue*, 189–91.

14. *Dialog of Catherine of Siena*, 125.

15. *Prayers of Catherine of Siena*, "Prayer 13," 127.

16. *The Dialogue of St. Catherine of Siena* (New York: Magisterium Press, 2015).

17. *Prayers of Catherine of Siena*, "Prayer 1," 5.

Week 4: St. Hildegard of Bingen

1. Carmen Acevedo Butcher, *St. Hildegard of Bingen: Doctor of the Church* (Brewster, MA: Paraclete Press, 2013), 48.

2. Francis, "Message of His Holiness Pope Francis to the Women's Consultation Group of the Pontifical Council for Culture on the Occasion of the Webinar 'Women Read Pope Francis,'" Libreria Editrice Vaticana, October 7, 2020, https://www.vatican.va/content/francesco/en/messages/pont-messages/2020/documents/papa-francesco_20201007_messaggio-consultafemminile-cultura.html.

3. Butcher, *St. Hildegard of Bingen*, 31.

4. Benedict XVI, "Proclaiming Saint Hildegard of Bingen, Professed Nun of the Order of Saint Benedict, a Doctor of the Universal Church," Libreria Editrice Vaticana, October 7, 2012, sec. 7, https://www.vatican.va/content/benedict-xvi/en/apost_letters/documents/hf_ben-xvi_apl_20121007_ildegarda-bingen.html.

5. Hildegard of Bingen, *Songs*, 3, as quoted in Sheryl A. Kujawa-Holbrook, trans. and annot., *Hildegard of Bingen: Essential Writings and Chants of a Christian Mystic—Annotated & Explained* (Woodstock, VT: SkyLight Paths, 2016), 101.

6. *Hildegard of Bingen: Selected Writings*, trans. Mark Atherton (New York: Penguin Books, 2001), 24.

7. Hildegard of Bingen, *Scivias*, trans. Mother Columba and Jane Bishop (Mahwah, NJ: Paulist Press, 1990), 489–90.

8. "Special Prayers by St. Hildegard von Bingen and Prayer for her Intercession—Patron of Music, Medicine, Theology," Catholic News World, September 17, 2018, www.catholicnewsworld.com/2018/09/special-prayers-by-st-hildegard-von.html.

9. *Hildegard of Bingen: Selected Writings*, 95.

10. Hildegard of Bingen, *Cause and Cure*, as quoted in Kujawa-Holbrook, *Hildegard of Bingen*, 99.

11. *Hildegard of Bingen: Selected Writings*, 105.

12. This prayer was used for Earth Day, 1990. From: Interfaith Declarations and Worship Observance Resources; The North American Conference on Religion and Ecology; 5 Thomas Circle, NW, Washington, DC, 20005.

13. *Hildegard of Bingen: Selected Writings*, antiphon 15, "Spiritus sanctus vivificans vita," antiphon 16, "Caritas abundant," and antiphon 17, "O gloriosissimi," 120–21.

14. Hildegard of Bingen, *Scivias* (Book Three, Vision Thirteen, 14), 534.

15. Hildegard of Bingen, "*Laus Trinitati*," LyricsTranslate.com, accessed August 23, 2021, https://lyricstranslate.com.

16. *Hildegard of Bingen: Selected Writings*, 58–61.

17. Hildegard of Bingen, *Scivias*, 429–30.

Vinita Hampton Wright is an award-winning author and workshop and retreat leader who served as a book editor for more than thirty years. She retired as managing editor at Loyola Press in 2021.

She is the author of a number of books, including *The Soul Tells a Story*, *The Art of Spiritual Writing*, and *The St. Teresa of Avila Prayer Book*. Her novel, *Velma Still Cooks in Leeway*, won a Logos Book Award for fiction, and *Christianity Today* honored her book *Dwelling Places* as the best fiction of 2007.

Wright earned a bachelor's degree in music education from Pittsburg State University in Kansas and a master's degree in communications from Wheaton College in Illinois. She also earned a certificate in spiritual direction from the Institute of Pastoral Studies at Loyola University Chicago. Wright previously worked as a teacher and musician in both the United States and abroad.

Wright lives in northwest Arkansas with her husband, James.

AVE

AVE MARIA PRESS

Founded in 1865, Ave Maria Press,
a ministry of the Congregation of
Holy Cross, is a Catholic publishing
company that serves the spiritual and
formative needs of the Church and its
schools, institutions, and ministers;
Christian individuals and families; and
others seeking spiritual nourishment.

For a complete listing of titles from

Ave Maria Press

Sorin Books

Forest of Peace

Christian Classics

visit avemariapress.com